INVESTING IN FINE WINE

INVESTING

= *in* =

FINE WINE

HOW TO BUY, SELL, *and* PROFIT

from THE WORLD'S MOST

DELICIOUS ASSET

====

ALEX ANDRAWES

with DARREN SCOTT

INVESTING IN FINE WINE

*How to Buy, Sell, and Profit from
the World's Most Delicious Asset*

ISBN 978-1-61961-636-3 *Paperback*

978-1-61961-635-6 *Ebook*

CONTENTS

FOREWORD

BY TUCKER MAX

———

I have to warn you: *I am not objective.*

I'm a client of Alex's. I've bought an insane amount of (awesome) wine from him.

Even more important, I'm his friend. We hang out all the time, and predictably, we drink a lot of expensive wine together (he even buys sometimes).

Alex asked me to write the foreword to his book, not because I'm his friend, but instead because he knew I'd tell you the truth.

(I'm kind of famous for doing that—being the guy who will say the things everyone thinks, but no one says. For real, I wrote three pretty famous books that did exactly that.)

So that's my job here: to tell you exactly what to expect from this book, who should read it, and why Alex wrote it.

First off, you should expect the best and most up-to-date information about investing in fine wine that exists (at least in book form). There are very few books on this subject that I can find (maybe two decent ones), and the good ones are old. They explain the basics of wine investing really well, but don't account for the massive changes that social media and the Internet have created in that field.

Alex is on top of all of that, and in fact, his strategies are so cutting-edge and user-friendly because they account for, and take advantage of, those changes. This book pulls back the curtain and talks about wine investing in a way no one else ever has, simply because most wine people are behind the times with the digital world.

Second, you shouldn't read this unless you are really serious about investing in wine. This book is only for those people. It's not about the "status signaling" aspect of wine. Alex does not mess around, and he has none of the snobbish pretention that so many people in the wine business have.

Like anyone who really knows his business, he doesn't care that much about appearances, because he has substance and he delivers results. This book is for people who want to cut through all the bullshit and get to the core facts that matter when you are investing in wine.

Third, Alex wrote the book because he wants clients for his business. Even though Alex is a hugely successful wine broker, he is always looking to add smart collectors to his client list.

But not just any clients. Alex wants clients who think like he does. Clients who are serious about making money. Clients who will listen to his (fantastic) advice. And perhaps most importantly, clients who are in this for the right reasons and don't need to be pandered to. Alex wrote this book to appeal to those people only—the ones who would make awesome clients for him, and with whom he would work well.

Alex is awesome at what he does, and he wants to work with people who are just as awesome at what they do.

And that is ultimate reason to read this book—to see what it looks like when someone who is at the top of his field pulls the curtain back to explain how he does it.

Alex does that, and it's incredible to see.

PART ONE

WHY WINE CAN BE A GREAT INVESTMENT

WHY READ THIS BOOK?

There are many books by much better writers who eloquently explore the love of wine. I'm a wine broker and wine investor, not a wine writer. This book is exclusively about a subject I know very well: how to invest in wine.

Like Tucker so directly explained to you in the foreword, I'm not going to explain how to sip wine, or tell you what decanting is, or explain why vintages are so important in tasting wine. Make no mistake, I love wine. I love smelling it, I love drinking it, and I love enjoying it with friends. I love learning about it and going to vineyards and tasting the grapes. I love everything about wine.

Though I love wine and investing in wine, I do not confuse the two. They are completely different and require entirely different approaches. I never let my love of wine cloud my judgment about investing in wines.

WHY INVEST
IN WINE?

On the surface, buying fine wine as an investment—as one would with real estate or a mutual fund—seems strange to many people. After all, it's made for you to drink, it has a limited life span, and it's so fragile that it needs to be stored correctly at all times or it can quickly become worthless. How could this be an investable asset?

Despite all this, wine can be a very profitable investment when you use the correct approach, especially if you're working with an experienced broker or expert. In fact, wine as an asset class has been one of the best-performing assets of the past twenty years (and many people now realize this, which is why so many people have asked me to write this book).

In recent years, people in the broader financial industry have woken up to the immense investment potential of rare wine. They've noticed that the value of a bottle of, say, Domaine Leflaive Montrachet Grand Cru, stored in excellent condition, has generally outperformed the Dow Jones and FTSE 100 over time. Wine, after all, is a product with very high demand yet a limited supply that only shrinks as time passes and corks pop open.

As a result, some investment firms are creating wine funds. In Asia, there's the Bordeaux Wine Bank, and in London you'll find the Fine Wine Investment Fund and Watermark Fine Wine, to name a few. With these investments, you're never actually taking possession of a bottle of wine. Instead, the funds themselves buy, sell, and store the assets. For you, the fund is just a way to diversify your portfolio and potentially profit from the wine market. It won't improve what's in your wine cellar.

Before I go any further, I should clarify something. For most of this book, when I refer to wine, I usually mean bottles that sell for anywhere from $200 to the tens of thousands of dollars. Bottles in this price range are generally called rare or collectible wines, and they're the most worthy ones for investment purposes. Meanwhile, bottles that sell between $50 and $200 are generally considered fine wines and can also be investable. Bottles that sell for prices below that category are often referred to as consumer wines, are not investable assets (you just drink these wines, and usually quickly upon release).

What sets a rare wine apart from fine wine or consumer wine are the prestige of the producer, the quality of the vintage year, and the scarcity of the product. Considerations are made about what region of the world it's produced in, how many cases are produced, whether it's made on the estate, where the grapes were grown, and how the wine was vinified and aged. What also sets it apart are the past results of the winemaker, how long that winemaker has been in business, and whether the wine was produced in an exceptional harvest year.

The more of these criteria a particular wine meets, the more desirable and valuable it is. Specific rare wine vintages get significantly pricier over time as people start drinking them and the supply around the world shrinks. Consumer wines, by contrast, are generally more mass-produced and meant to be consumed within a five- to seven-year window, so they generally don't appreciate over time. Fine wines fall somewhere in the middle.

What sets wine apart from other collectibles that are bought and sold as investments—, like baseball cards, stamps, and coins—is its history of price stability. If you buy a pack of baseball cards, the contents are practically worthless once you take them out of the packaging. Their value stays that way for many years, until they grow scarcer or the card of a particular player becomes more desirable according to his history and fame—and then you can finally recoup the original cost. Then, some day— decades and decades later—some of those cards might be worth some real money. Their price is also more erratic because they rely on highly volatile collecting trends and emotions like nostalgia. For instance, some baseball cards from the 1960s are worth less today than during the collecting craze that took hold in the United States during the 1980s and 1990s.

The market for postage stamps has experienced the same fluctuations as well. There are a prized few that have a value of $50,000 to $100,000 apiece. One, the Inverted Jenny, is worth close to a million dollars. Issued in the United States in 1918, it displayed a biplane upside down, as a result of a printing error. Only one hundred were accidentally released, and the rest were recalled and destroyed.

Coins are subject to similar variations. They do rise in value, but they don't experience tremendous growth in value unless the metal they're made of—like gold or silver—jumps dramatically.

One of the benefits investors find in collecting rare wine is the liquidity of it, so to speak. Converting a bottle to cash is relatively easy if you have a skilled broker. An investor might say, "It's time for me to write that check for my kid's college tuition," and it's simpler to sell some wine than to take a second mortgage on the house or unload larger assets. And in the past two decades, the value of rare wine has been on a rocket climb—with a few bumps along the way. The rise of the market for fine wine appeals to a more conservative investor looking for a steady return and an expected, manageable growth rate.

As with any investment, you need to know when to sell. Sometimes investors should hold on to a product because it's not at peak value due to, say, a temporary shift in taste preferences or popularity. Alternatively, a wine's window of drinkability may lie too far ahead into the future. At other times, investors hoping for top dollar might have the urge to hang on to a product too long, only to find that the opportunity to sell at a high price has passed. For many investors, owning a bottle of wine is as much an emotional investment as it is a financial one, and I understand that because I feel the same way. So the decision to sell a wine collection needs to be well thought out and often involves a very candid conversation about your motivations.

3

WHO SHOULD INVEST IN WINE?

To be a wine collector or investor, you do not need to be extremely knowledgeable at the start, or be part of some elite circle of aficionados who can identify a fine vintage at first sip. You should, however, be willing to learn over time so that you understand your purchasing decisions. You may not even need to drink wine, but I would highly recommend you have an appreciation for wine. Just as someone who's indifferent about sports probably shouldn't bother collecting baseball cards, if you don't salivate over a bottle of Château Lafite-Rothschild (or any other elite producer), you're probably better served focusing on more traditional investments. Why spend your time learning about an asset that isn't exciting to you?

I've found through my experience that there are generally three types of wine collectors, and only two should be investors.

The first type are people who drink everything they buy—they are collectors and not investors. They're not interested in selling at all, but just want to consume the great artwork of an exceptional vintage. Generally these people are epicureans. They will spend top dollar on a fine meal and will spare no expense on a fine bottle of wine. Let me be clear: not all of these people are rich. After all, isn't wine meant for enjoyment through drinking?

In the second category are the combined collectors and investors. They might purchase twelve bottles of a given wine in order to drink three and sell nine. With the profit they make on the sales, they're basically able to pop the corks on those three bottles for pretty close to free.

For example, if you bought a three-pack of Screaming Eagle Cabernet Sauvignon 2012 on release, with shipping included, you paid $2,792, producing a net bottle price of $930.67. At today's prices of $2,249 per bottle, if you sold it to a broker, you could probably achieve a net of $1,799 per bottle. If you drank one bottle and sold the other two, you would be able to collect $3,598, giving you a free bottle of Screaming Eagle and $800 in profit.

In the third category are pure investors. They don't open anything. Their wine purchases are basically widgets sitting in wooden boxes in their wine cellars—or most likely sitting in temperature-controlled wine storage warehouses. They wait, wait, wait, and after some length of time—say ten years—when the vintage's drinking window opens, they sell it. The only basic costs incurred to them are the utility or rent bills to keep the wine as fresh as possible and under the right conditions, which they more than recoup in their sales. They're usually people with highly diversified portfolios who are fed up with Wall Street. They amass scarce, highly collectible objects—like coins, art, and fine wine—as an alternative investment.

Pure wine investors can often look at holding on to a bottle over a shorter term—though they're not wine flippers. California vineyards offer excellent release prices of new vintages to valued customers on their mailing lists, and a shrewd investor will buy an allocation from somewhere like Screaming Eagle in Napa or Sine Qua Non in Ventura County, hold it, and then sell it down the line after it appreciates in price.

When I work with clients who see wine solely as an investment, I advise them to think of it as a ten-year play. Sometimes it may be one year—based on what opportunities present themselves—or three to five years, particularly with Burgundy, which appreciates at a higher early rate. But with Napa or Bordeaux wines, you're looking at a decade before you see the right level of return in order to sell. If you're looking for liquidity, and one- to three-year investments, wine is probably not for you.

There is no right or wrong way to collect wine. You can be any of the three types of collectors. The important thing is that you know which category you fall into, and you invest in wine accordingly. The next part of the book goes into detail about how to invest in wine the right way.

PART TWO

HOW TO INVEST IN WINE

4

WINE-INVESTING BASICS

If you want to use wine as an investment, the realistic amount that you should be starting with is no less than $10,000 a year. That's a bare minimum. Most people invest more. For example, the majority of my clients at Estate Wine Brokers put $25,000 to $50,000 per year into wine.

Of those, roughly 50 percent are in it to drink for free. They just want to drink very high-end wine for free, or close to free. So, for example, they'll buy six bottles, drink two, and sell four. They tend to spend $10,000 to $25,000 a year.

Then there are definitely people who are in essence operating wine funds (or literally operating them for family offices or groups of wealthy friends), and they will buy allocations of ten to twenty-five cases at a time, multiple times a year. Those people are typically spending $50,000 (or in many instances, much, much more than that).

If you are investing $10,000 to $25,000 a year with the help of a great wine broker, over a decade, you can expect the return on that investment to be between 12 percent and 14 percent per year. That is what my clients have gotten in the past, and that ROI is common for the high-level wine brokers. If you're just doing it yourself (and are skilled or lucky), or you've got a decent or okay (but not great) wine broker, then you can expect somewhere between 5 percent and 10 percent per year, still a very solid ROI.

Those returns are of course only for the people who are strict investors, not the ones who are investing to drink "for free." For those investors, the return is being able to drink expensive wine "for free." And of course, for those people, it could be argued that the rooms they are going to be in because they are drinking those high-end wines will certainly open doors for them, and lead to other opportunities that will be useful in their lives. But that is a nonmonetary return—and though it's important to many people, only you can say if that is worth the investment to you. For many of my clients, the wine is the way into relationships and deals that are worth far, far more than the cost of the bottle.

Investing in wine means, at its core, that you buy wine and store it until the price goes up, and then you sell it. That is obvious. But what many people don't understand is that there are two basic ways to invest in wine: use a wine broker to manage the process, or manage the process yourself. I will explain how both ways work and how to do each one.

5

A GREAT BROKER IS KEY TO WINE INVESTING

Wine brokers are similar to stockbrokers, or any other sort of investment professionals. Their job is to have deep knowledge of their field, recommend which wines you should invest in, help facilitate the purchase, and then take a fee on the transaction.

You might be thinking right now that the world is changing quite a bit, and many people don't need the services of many types of financial professionals. They are using platforms like E-Trade or software services like Wealthfront to do most of the work themselves, and therefore save money. Quite a bit of what used to be exclusively the realm of professionals is now "do-it-yourself."

That is all true, but wine brokers are unlike financial professionals in that they do work that is still very hard—if not impossible—to automate or do yourself. Because wine is a physical asset, highly depreciable, and very complicated to price and trade, and because there is no single market through which to trade wine, a wine broker must have a lot more specific knowledge and must be able to coordinate many more moving parts than many financial professionals (in the current day).

In the next chapter, I'll explain what they do, and you will see why this is very difficult (if not impossible) to replicate yourself.

6

WHAT IS A WINE BROKER, AND WHAT DO THEY DO?

At a basic level, a wine broker is someone who acts as a middleman between people selling fine (or rare) wine and people looking to buy fine wine. There are many wine brokers, but not many good ones, and it is crucial that you work with only with good wine brokers.

The difference between a good and bad wine broker is the difference between making 12-14 percent and nothing, or oftentimes losing money.

The following are the things a good wine broker does.

A good wine broker will have a liquor license and experience shipping wine all around the world. Shipping wine (or any alcohol) across state and national borders is fraught with legal and regulatory compliance issues, and must be done right. There are many ways to do it wrong, and doing it wrong can result in fines, confiscation, or in extreme cases, exposure to criminal charges.

A good wine broker will have a well-maintained physical facility (with power backups) to properly store wine and ensure it does not spoil.

A good wine broker will have a large and varied clientele, both as a signal that the broker is good at their job and to ensure they have both a constant supply of wine for their clients looking to buy, and a large pool of buyers to provide liquidity to clients looking to sell.

A good wine broker will have extensive experience in many different parts of the wine industry. They will know the important local knowledge and industry gossip and be able to see major changes coming early enough to act on them.

A good wine broker will have deep and long-term contacts with auction houses, wineries, and other wine brokers, all over the world. The broker will personally know many of the major players and be able to connect with anyone else quickly, if necessary.

A good wine broker will have impeccable ethical standards, a meticulous reputation, and expert experience in confirming provenance and authenticity of fine wine (this is *very* important, as you will see later in the book).

And most importantly, a good wine broker will have excellent understanding of all aspects of wine, especially the commercial potential of fine wine. Quite frankly, the broker has to be an expert at what the market will pay for wine now, and an expert at predicting what the market will want to pay in the future. If there is one thing that separates the good from the great, this ability is it.

7

WHY A WINE BROKER MAKES WINE INVESTING EASY

Imagine managing all of those tasks yourself—on top of your normal job. I think you can see why there is no question that the easiest way to invest in wine is to use a wine broker.

The question is not whether you should you use a wine broker or not. Of course you should. The question is which wine broker you should use, and how to find the right one for you.

This is the hardest part about investing in wine: finding the right person to help you manage the process, so you will achieve your investment goals.

The first thing I would recommend is that you actually use *two* wine brokers, not just one. I am a wine broker, and I recommend this to my clients. This is mainly because the varied and distributed nature of the wine market makes it impossible for any one broker to be able to always meet all the needs of any one client.

In the next chapter, I will first explain how to select a wine broker, and then I will recommend some I think are top-notch.

8

HOW TO FIND AND SELECT A WINE BROKER

I have been in the wine business all my adult life, and I know, at least by reputation, all the major wine brokers in the country. When my friends come to me and ask how to find and select a wine broker to work with, this is how I recommend that they do it.

STEP 1: LOOK FOR EXPERIENCE

This is the easiest way to sort the real professionals from the fakers. Just ask: Who has been in the ultra-high-end, fine wine business for an extended period of time?

You do not necessarily want to use length of time as a wine broker as the only factor, or even the most important factor, but it should be the first thing you look at. What is their experience in high-end fine wine, both as a wine broker, and before becoming a wine broker?

How do you know someone has enough experience in high-end, fine wine?

The first and most obvious thing to look at is how long they've been a successful wine broker. That by itself is a *very* strong signal. This is because the wine broker business is entirely a relationship and reputation business. If a wine broker can stay in business for a long time, it means they have strong relationships with people and have done well by them. It also means that the broker has a long track record of doing a great job, and their reputation reflects that. Most of my business is by referrals, and the same is true for all good wine brokers.

But even if a wine broker been doing this for a while, you should still check their background. There is not a "right" thing to look for, but the following are the three things that should make you feel more confident in a wine broker's experience.

1. AUCTION HOUSE EXPERIENCE

If a wine broker has worked for one of the top five auction houses, that is a very good sign. The number-one house would be Hart Davis Hart. Then you have Sotheby's and Christie's, then Zachy's, and then Heritage. There are other auction houses; however, other auction houses have made some pretty serious mistakes in checking the provenance of wine. Those five have the best reputations.

Note on mistakes: What do I mean when I say "serious mistakes"? I mean these auction houses have been buying and selling and consigning counterfeit wines without really performing the basic level of provenance check, which I find to be a fatal flaw. Just because an auction house has been around for a long period of time, doesn't necessarily qualify them to be superior. What qualifies them to be superior is that they follow the customers' expectations and have never been flagged for selling counterfeit products.

2. HIGH-END RETAIL EXPERIENCE

Someone with experience at a retail house that specializes in super fine wine is also very good.

What's a retail house? A retail house is basically a wine store. For example, some of the high-end retail houses include K&L Wines, Wally's, Knightsbridge, Schneiders of Capitol Hill, BevMo!, BevMax, and Total Wine & More. There are many of these in the country; it would be exhausting to list them all.

What you are looking for is whether the broker has a lot of experience tasting and buying super-high-end, fine wines, and then selling these wines to actual people. You also want to look at the size of the retail outlet—or, I should say, the volume of high-end wine they sell. Costco sells an incredible volume of wine every year, but virtually none of it is high end or investable wine, so experience as the Costco wine buyer is not relevant to being a wine broker.

Compare that to a small wine store that specializes in wines over $100, has hundreds of repeat clients, and is where wineries and distributors like doing local tastings in that area. Working in a store like this will expose someone to a large amount of high-end wine and elite clientele, and give them experience in the exact skills a wine broker must have.

If someone works at a retail house that moves a lot of high-end wine, he or she becomes an expert in the most important aspect of wine: what people buy, and for what price.

3. MICHELIN STAR RESTAURANT EXPERIENCE

Working for Michelin star-rated restaurants also can expose someone to the requisite experience of tasting and selling super fine wine.

Be careful here, though—not all work at restaurants is the same. If you're looking for somebody who has worked at a fine wine restaurant, it would be more desirable to have somebody who is a trained sommelier, preferably with an advanced or Master Sommelier status, or a Master of Wine.

The downfall to hiring a sommelier from a restaurant to pick and choose your wine is that the sommelier may not have worked at the right restaurant, or they are just out to taste wine. Are they going to buy esoteric wines, or are they going to buy wines that will go up in value? Someone who buys wine for public consumption is not always looking for the same things as someone who buys wine as an investment.

STEP 2: TEST THEM TO ASSESS THEIR SKILLS

Most wine brokers you come across will pass Step 1, having experience. If they don't, remove them from consideration immediately.

But once you've found five to ten wine brokers who have experience, and they all seem credible, what do you do then? How do you pick?

I am going to recommend something that will seem obvious to anyone with financial experience, but which is somewhat controversial in the wine world. *I think you should test them, and make them prove they can pick winners before you do business with them.*

I am always willing to prove myself before someone decides to invest with me, and I would personally be very suspicious of anyone who balked at giving proof of their knowledge.

That being said, what most wine brokers will do is tell you that they have been successful, and they'll possibly refer you to clients who have made a lot of money with them. That's fine, and checking references is important (I go over this later on), but that is not what I am talking about here.

It does no good for someone to tell you that they picked successful wines in the past. Everyone knows an investment in La Tache fifteen years ago has had an amazing return. That doesn't really show you how they are going to help you going forward.

I recommend you ask your potential wine brokers
you how they will help YOU make money.

How do you do that? This is what I recommend to my friends:

Tell the wine broker that you would like to invest $10,000 a year in wine (or whatever amount you are comfortable with, but $10,000 is the minimum). Then ask the broker to give you a list of the wines he or she would recommend that you buy, and what price he or she would charge you. This is very similar to that stockbroker game that people play in school, where the teacher gives you $100,000 in Monopoly money, and you show what stocks you'd invest in.

The wine broker should come back to you with a list of about twenty-five to fifty wines, with prices (make sure that the broker provides you with a vintage of the wine as well).

Here is how you check the broker's recommendations. Go to the Wine Searcher website (www.wine-searcher.com). Upgrade to the pro version, and then look up each wine by typing in the name of wine, making sure you click on the proper vintage for each, and then clicking on the "market data" tab, which will show you the price history of that specific wine.

If somebody gives you a list of wines with flat price histories, that wine broker doesn't know what they're talking about. Even worse, if the prices of many of the wines are downhill, or if the broker gave you a list of wines that nobody's ever heard about, and are all very cheap. All these are very bad signs.

What you are looking for are wines that are not too expensive, probably in the $100 to $500 range, and have a history of rising prices, especially recently.

If you want to get more technical detail on a wine broker's recommendations, then what you could do is actually track auction data. You can find auction data on the Wine Market Journal website (www.winemarketjournal.com). That is the number-one site for tracking auction data; they are very good.

When you look at auction history, what you're looking at are the improvements in very specific categories. You are looking to see which of a wine broker's recommended wines actually performed at their highs or above their highs. That means those wines are hot and will probably keep rising in price. That's when you're catching a wave right before the swell. That's where you want to be.

But if their wines are selling at the low end of the ranges, it indicates that the market is soft for those wines.

I think that the difference between a good and a bad broker is how much they need to persuade you to buy. If a wine broker is pushing something on you, that's a bad sign. Really great wine doesn't need to be pushed. You can see the demand in the prices.

Look at what they're recommending to you specifically. Are they selling you wine that is already old? Is it already at its peak? Or are they selling you wine that has a certain amount of window left over so that it meets your threshold? Are they listening to you?

If you say, "Look, I'm going to buy $10,000 a year worth of wine for ten years. That's $100,000, and in year ten I want to sell all of it," then you want to make sure you're buying wine that has a drink window of at least ten to twenty years. Otherwise, nobody's going to buy your expired wine. That is just expensive vinegar.

Another way to test a wine broker's skills is to ask: "Right now, what are your five to ten favorite wines under the radar investments?"

A good wine broker will always have a few producers they are watching, that are likely to break out, and if you are potentially going to be a client, the broker should tell you who those producers are. Is the wine broker hearing any back chatter in the sommelier community on specific producers who could make a wine that would last fifteen to twenty-five years? Is there anybody there that the broker knows of who has still got great value, on whom allocations are starting to tighten up a bit? Does the broker know of wines you can still get, but on which the allocations are tightening up? That's when you know there's demand behind the wine.

I'll give you a great example of a wave I caught early on, and which most good wine brokers know about by now: Rhone. Most Burgundy and Bordeaux have seen their major growth spurts, but the high-end Rhone Valley wines are nearly as good and still drastically underpriced relative to those other two regions. I have been buying large allocations of high-end fine Rhone Valley wines like Château Rayas for quite a while, and my clients have seen excellent returns, which are only accelerating.

STEP 3: CHECK THEIR PRICES

As you are checking the price trends of the wines your potential wine brokers recommend, you should also be

checking the actual prices they are quoting you.
look up every wine on their lists on Wine Search
Wine Market Journal, look to see if their prices are ﹍ ﹍
proper levels. If they are within 10 percent of the lowest
three confirmed price quotes, then that's about right. If
they are consistently higher than that, something is off.

Remember, if you are going to be buying $10,000 worth
of wine a year or more, your wine broker should be giving
you good prices, close to the best you can find on the
wider market.

STEP 4: CHECK THEIR REPUTATION
AND THEIR CLIENT REFERENCES

At this point, you should only have three to five finalists
left, for two spots. Now it's time to dig into the details of
their business.

A good broker should be able to give you very good references when you ask. And not other people in the industry.
They should be actual clients, people like you.

Furthermore, you should check each broker's reputation
online. This takes a little detective work, but it's not hard.
There are a lot of forums that have information about wine
brokers. For example, I would start with Wine Berserkers

(www.wineberserkers.com/forum) or Wine Spectator (http://forums.winespectator.com), which are the two forum authorities.

Go into the "buying and selling" parts of the forum. You can search for the wine brokers' names and see what other people have said about them in the past. Or you can sign up and basically post something asking, "I'm thinking of doing business with this person. Have you done business with this person before, and would you give this person a good rating?" If somebody does not think that person has a good reputation, that person will definitely get flagged and you will know.

Those two forums are where you can immediately go and check, and you're going to get some response. If you get no response, then maybe you just have to do a little bit more digging, or maybe that person is not very established in the business.

STEP 5: CHECK THEIR LIQUOR LICENSE

Another thing that you want to double-check is whether they have a liquor license. If you're going to physically touch a bottle of wine (in the United States), and you're going to make it publicly available for purchase, you have to have a license.

DO NOT skip this step.

Why? This tells you that the person has a high degree of being a legitimate operator and has a clean history. If you get a liquor license, you have to have a clean criminal background check. If you've been arrested for a felony, theft, or something else, it'll show up, and you will not be allowed to get a liquor license.

If they have a liquor license, there is a governmental authority you can appeal to if any dispute arises. And they *must* take this seriously, much more seriously than even a civil lawsuit. A revocation of a wine broker's liquor license is a direct threat to their livelihood, so the broker will not do anything to jeopardize that.

If they do NOT have a liquor license, then you only have conventional legal methods, which are often not enough.

I say this from experience. I got screwed by two "wine brokers" who were operating without a liquor license. Both are documented in the Wine Spectator forum, actually, but I will quickly tell the stories here.

The first was a gentleman who was out of Scottsdale, Arizona. He had allocations of Marcassin, and he sold the same allocation to ten different people. He took the money, and then when his scam was figured out, he promised to pay everybody who didn't get their allocation. But he paid them out over a period of six months, so he basically took an interest-free loan from me and eight other people. But at least I got my money back in that case.

Then there was another guy, named Joe Le (aka JVL Consulting or Thiet Van Le). He's a professional con man. He did five or six seamless transactions with me, all legit. Then he went to a restaurant, took pictures of two bottles of Romanee Conti, and tried to sell them to me. Because I'd done business with him, I thought I could trust him. But he took my money and never sent me the wine. He's still out there wearing slick suits that I paid for. Yes, I pursued him criminally, but the amount I had paid was so small that the FBI was not interested, and the state police basically dropped the ball.

Learn from my mistake. Make sure you deal with professionals only, and a liquor license is a must for a professional.

STEP 6: CHECK THEIR FACILITIES

The last step is to check a broker's facilities. If possible, you should literally visit them. If you are going to be buying and possibly storing wine with a broker for years, you should ensure they have proper wine storage facilities.

You want to make sure the storage area is dry and has redundant power backups. This is incredibly important. Furthermore, you want to make sure they can take delivery for you. And their storage fees should be very small for a client. Cheap storage is typically about twenty-five to thirty-five cents per case per month, which is not expensive. That's worth every penny, considering that a good storage warehouse has redundant power systems.

Furthermore, storing your wine with them ensures that you can confirm the provenance when it comes time to sell.

AN EXAMPLE OF A GOOD WINE BROKER TEST

If someone approached me as a wine broker and asked me to go through these tests, here are the answers I would give them at the time of the writing of this book (March 2017).

This is how I would recommend allocating a $10,000 investment:

WINE NAME	VINTAGE	PRICE 3/17, 1 BOTTLE	TOTAL INVESTMENT
Château La Mission Haut Brion	2005	$450	$900
Château Angelus	2009	$349	$698
Domaine Fourrier Clos St. Jacques	2015	$429	$858
Domaine du Comte Liger-Belair Vosne-Romanee Clos du Château Monopole	2014	$300	$600
Domaine George Noëllat Grands Echezeaux	2015	$250	$500
Scarecrow	2014	$400	$800
Futo Oakville Cabernet	2012	$275	$550
JL Chave Hermitage	2010	$425	$850
Henri Bonneau Cuvee Celestin	2010	$500	$1,000
Château Rayas	2009	$525	$1,050
Aldo Conterno Monfortino	2008	$585	$1,170
Elio Altare Cannubi Barolo	2012	$150	$300
Vietti Villero, Barolo Riserva DOCG	2007	$345	$690
Pian dell'Orino Bassolino di Sopra Riserva Brunello	2010	$119	$238
		TOTAL	$10,474

I would predict that in three to five years, you could drink one of these wines, sell one of each of them, and literally drink for free or, at most, at 20 percent of the original total cost. The goal would be to buy twelve and sell nine, but that cash outlay would be around $62,500 if you were to buy at retail low.

Still, I think it would be fair to say that you could possibly buy this for 10–15 percent less than the prices posted above if you bought the wines from a broker or a trusted source. I would certainly ask for provenance on all of these purchases.

The following is a list of fifteen specific wines or producers that I am currently recommending my clients buy (and I am also buying them personally as well). I make no guarantees, of course. I am just telling you some areas where I see heat coming in the next five to ten years:

1. Château La Mission Haut Brion (2005, 2009, 2010)
2. Château Angelus (2009, 2010)
3. Domaine Fourrier Clos St. Jacques (2012, 2014, 2015)
4. Comte Liger Belair (any Grand Cru or Premier Cru wines from 2012, 2015)
5. Domaine George Noëllat Grands Echezeaux (2012, 2014, 2015)
6. Scarecrow (2012, 2013, 2014)
7. Futo Oakville Cabernet (2012, 2013)
8. Ridge Monte Bello (2012, 2013)
9. JL Chave Hermitage (2009, 2012)
10. Henri Bonneau Cuvee Celestin (2007, 2009, 2010)
11. Château Rayas (2005, 2007, 2009, 2012)
12. Aldo Conterno Monfortino (2006, 2008, 2012)
13. Elio Altare Cannubi Barolo (2006, 2012)
14. Vietti Villero, Barolo Riserva DOCG, Italy (2004, 2006)
15. Pian dell'Orino Bassolino di Sopra Riserva Brunello (2010, 2012)

WHERE TO START: TRUSTED WINE BROKERS

When my clients ask me for referrals to other wine brokers to use (in addition to my company Estate Wine Brokers, www.estatewinebrokers.com), this is the list I give them.

They are not the only good wine brokers out there, but they are the ones I can personally vouch for, as I have done business with them for years and all have good reputations in the broader wine community:

- Hart Davis Hart (www.hdhwine.com)
- Benchmark Wines (www.benchmarkwine.com)
- Chai Consulting (www.chaiconsulting.com)
- RL Liquid Assets (rlliquidassets.com)

9

THE HARD WAY TO INVEST IN WINE: DO IT YOURSELF

The hard way to invest in wine is to do it by yourself, without a broker. I would not recommend this to anyone.

That being said, just because it's hard, does not mean it's impossible. You can do it, and I am going to show you a way to make it much easier on yourself than most people think it is.

Most people think that the only way to invest in wine is to have deep knowledge of wines and the wine industry. The regions, the producers, the winemakers, the grapes—the amount of knowledge is overwhelming and takes years to acquire. If you want to be wine broker, that's true—you have to know all of that, and there is no way around it.

But there is a way to invest in wine and not have to learn about all of this. That is the method I will focus on here: how to get the maximal return for the minimal effort in wine investing when you do it yourself.

STEP 1: START WITH THE TOP 100 MOST SEARCHED-FOR WINES

Go to the Wine Searcher website (www.wine-searcher.com), upgrade to the pro version ($49 a year), and search for the top one hundred "most searched for" wines. These are the wines that people are searching for the most, in the largest wine price database on the Internet.

STEP 2: FOCUS ON $100 TO $299

Get rid of anything over $300. Those wines (probably) have very little appreciation left, or if they do, you won't be able to tell which will go up and which won't without deep wine knowledge.

Get rid of everything under $100. Those wines are (probably) not going to get much more expensive.

That obviously leaves you with wines from $100 to $299 in value. This is where you will find value.

STEP 3: KEEP ONLY THE NOTEWORTHY VARIETALS AND REGIONS

Now, keep only the wines from one of these regions:

- Bordeaux (red and white)
- Burgundy (red only)
- Napa Valley (Cabernet Sauvignon or red blends only)
- Super Tuscans (red only)
- Rhone Valley (red only)
- Piedmont (Barolo only)

STEP 4: FIND THE MOMENTUM BUYS

Now the real work begins. Take a look at each of the wines you're left with individually, and then look at their price history. You can find this in Wine Searcher as well, conveniently in graph form.

What you are looking for are the ones that are basically on the incline. Which wines have seen their prices go up recently? Those are the ones you want.

If you want to get more technical detail on their price movements, and be more certain of their momentum, then track auction data. You can find auction data on the Wine Market Journal website (www.winemarketjournal.com).

What you're looking for are wines performing at their highs or above their high's in auctions. That means they are hot and will probably keep rising in price. That's when you're catching a wave right before the swell. That's where you want to be.

But if the wines you are looking at are selling at the low end of the ranges, that indicates that the market is soft for those wines.

STEP 5: FIND THE RIGHT VINTAGES

Now you have wines that you know are very popular with people, that are in demand but still reasonably priced and with room for appreciation, from regions that have a long history of high demand and high prices, and are rising in price. There is only one step left: check the expiration date.

Remember, to effectively invest in wine, you must sell it before it "expires." This means you need to buy wine relatively young, hold it for five to fifteen years, and then sell it at its peak. So you need to research the vintages on

Wine Searcher, and make sure the years you are buying are good ones that will last for the required time.

Take Napa wines, for example. On Wine Searcher you can see that the best vintages over the last ten years are 2007, 2012, and 2013. Those wines will last the longest, many of them for fifteen to twenty years, and sometimes—as in the case of Dominus or Ridge Monte Bello—they could last twenty-five years or more. Those are the years you want to focus on.

STEP 6: REPEAT UNTIL YOU'VE BOUGHT YOUR BUDGET

It is possible that the top one hundred most searched wines won't give you enough options, so expand your search until you have found enough wines to satisfy your budget. You may even want to do the top one hundred wines in each category that I outlined for you, or maybe even the top two hundred in each category. It all depends on your budget.

Now, you wait and watch. If you made the right choices, your investments will appreciate quite nicely. And the best part is that you don't have to learn much about wine.

PART THREE

THE BASICS OF UNDERSTANDING WINE AS AN INVESTMENT

HOW WINE BECAME
AN INVESTMENT

Drinking wine from a box is one thing, but have you ever heard of a wine brick? During Prohibition, which was enacted in 1920, that's how California vineyards worked around federal laws and sold alcoholic beverages. Wineries would ship tightly packed bricks of grapes, concocted so that consumers could just add water and make their own wine at home—which was legal to do.

The only problem was that varieties like Pinot Noir and Cabernet Sauvignon were too fragile to survive being put into bricks and shipped across the country. So many farmers dug out their old vines and replanted their fields with the hardier Alicante Bouschet variety, which lasted longer. The result was a lot of really terrible wine, and even worse, a change in American perception of—and tastes for—wine.

These bricks were one of the many unfortunate, unintended consequences of Prohibition. Another was the devastation of tax revenues on the local and national level. At that time, in the United States, the concept of an income tax was still new, and state and federal governments derived most of their money from taxing liquor. It was estimated that the State of New York received 75 percent of its revenue from alcohol taxes. For the federal government, these taxes were second only to customs duties as the largest source of revenue. When all of this money disappeared from government coffers—on top of the cost to enforce the law—income taxes were sent sky high.

After Prohibition was finally repealed in 1933, the damage was done. Income taxes remained, and individual states were handed the right to control alcohol production and consumption within their borders, which they did heavily. Most created a three-tiered system, distinctly separating producers, distributors, and retailers. This arrangement gave states full control over the alcoholic beverage industry. The problem was that each state crafted its laws somewhat differently—usually the result of heavy lobbying from different powerful families or corporations in different regions, intended to tilt the playing field in their favor.

In turn, a jumble of conflicting laws arose across the country, which to this day makes doing business at times confusing and burdensome. For example, Pennsylvania and Utah monopolize all distribution and retail sales of alcohol within their borders. Michigan only controls distribution, and seventeen states, including North Carolina, New Hampshire, and Idaho, exert either partial or complete control over retail sales. In Oklahoma, liquor stores are independently owned, but they can't sell anything but alcoholic beverages—not even a corkscrew. The best state that doesn't heavily regulate some form of a three-tiered system is Washington, DC, which eliminated its state liquor stores in 2011.

As a result, there's no such thing today as a free market in the alcoholic beverage industry in the United States. Some people say that there needs to be some regulation in the business. I agree. Alcohol can be too easily abused if there aren't some limits and controls, and it shouldn't be accessible to minors. But the complexity of fifty states enforcing fifty different sets of legal codes hurts everybody—especially the smaller producers. There's no way a boutique winery who owns, say, seven acres can sell enough product to afford to fill out paperwork and hire the lawyers to understand the legal complexities for selling product in twenty states, let alone fifty. This producer also can't always get their wine distributed by the powerful distributors, because their returns are relatively low and marketing dollars to support the brand just aren't there.

These days, boutique wineries might decide to sell directly to consumers, which is legal in some—but not all—states. Such a setup requires a lot of legwork on the part of the owners, to make sure their products are being placed in the right restaurants and in the cellars of the right, influential wealthy people to create a buzz and have others say, "Ooh, I've never had that wine; I'd like to get a bottle of it." But in the process of doing this work, the owners need to hire people to make their wine, tend to the vines, perform the administrative duties, and manage sales. It can take more than ten years for a boutique to begin to turn a profit this way. Whether you own a winery, distribution company, or retail outlet, it is a minimum of five to seven years to achieve profitability. The reason for this certainly derives from the various hands that wine must pass through as a result of the three-tier system.

As states slowly update their laws to take down some of the roadblocks to the sale of alcoholic beverages—in a nod to the growing trend of boutique wineries and craft-beer breweries—the direct-to-consumer model is getting more popular, despite the legal barriers. In the wine industry in the United States, direct-to-consumer sales accounted for more than $3.5 billion in revenue last year, or roughly 10 percent of all domestic wine sales.

Returning, for a moment, to the unintended consequences of Prohibition, the segment of the alcohol industry that struggled the most after the repeal was the wine business. Beer and liquor rebounded relatively quickly. But consumer tastes had largely been turned off wine—thanks in part to those terrible wine bricks—and the vineyards were unequipped to make quality products because they had replaced the vines growing top-notch varieties with Alicante Bouschet.

A newly planted Pinot Noir vine needs to grow for at least ten years before it produces grapes with quality flavor, and the thirsty American public was impatient. Filling the void were industrial winemakers who produced substandard products, and as a result, turned off the public at large. It's estimated that by the early 1940s, American wine consumption had dropped to half of what it was prior to Prohibition.

The American wine market didn't slowly start to rebound until the late 1960s, when the literal fruits of vintners' labors to grow better grapes and relearn how to make quality wine began to pay off. In the decade that followed, California wines finally began to emerge to prominence and challenge even the products by classic French winemakers. Consumers began to take notice, both in the United States and abroad.

Some of this shift was fueled by critics, particularly the American wine critic Robert Parker. He was a lawyer from Maryland who began writing about wine on the side, starting in 1975, at the age of twenty-eight. He had fallen in love with wine during a college visit to his girlfriend studying in France. Parker had an idea of creating a consumer's guide that rated wine quality. So, in 1978, he did it by publishing the first issue of the *Wine Advocate* and distributing it to mailing lists he bought from major wine retailers.

Until that time, wine reviews weren't readily available to the public, and they were usually tainted by conflicts of interest in the industry, since reviewers often shared close ties to the producers. Parker popularized the 100-point rating system, which became easy for the public to understand, and encouraged wine drinkers to become more discerning. His emergence also set the table for the most historic moment in California winemaking history, which is now called the Judgment of Paris.

In 1976, noted wine critic Steven Spurrier organized a blind taste test in Paris, with French judges selected to assess the quality of the top California Cabernet Sauvignons and Chardonnays against the best Bordeaux and Burgundy wines. Each entry was to be graded on a scale of twenty points, with no specific criteria. In the end, American entries won top grades in the red and white wine categories. The French press ignored the event after the results came down. But a reporter from *Time Magazine* was there and told the world.

From there, interest in American wine took off. California winery owners such as Robert Mondavi and Joe Heitz began accumulating massive parcels of land thanks to improved market conditions, and the production of premium wines grew exponentially. Tastes in the United States gradually extended beyond jug wines, and the demand for premium wines increased.

Culture shifts played a role in the industry's growth as well. James Bond appeared on the big screen, drinking Dom Perignon instead of the cliché "martini, shaken, but not stirred." Characters in other movies were requesting specific wines, glamorizing expensive vintages across the country and world. In the 1980s, the extraordinary strength of the dollar against European currencies motivated vineyards to ship their products to America, where they could profitably sell their fine and rare wines at advantageous prices.

The credibility of a small handful of wine reviewers took on even greater weight and credibility as the years passed after the Judgment of Paris. In addition to Robert Parker's *Wine Advocate*, consumers began relying on the judgment of publications like *Wine Spectator*, *Wine Enthusiast*, and *International Wine Cellar*. These publications became so incredibly powerful that they could make or break a wine, or winery, based upon its scores. The reviewers also solidified the credibility and reputation of the small handful of winemakers who consistently received high ratings. People began to know that the name Château Lafite-Rothschild meant high quality.

The wine market got an added, welcome boost from the incredible growing seasons and harvests in France in 1982 and 1983. The winemakers of Bordeaux had suffered tremendously in the previous decade. Conditions have to be perfect for a great vintage—with the right combination of sun, rain, warmth, and humidity—and they just weren't in the 1970s. Across the board, you won't find an innovative vintage for Bordeaux from the days of disco. You might be able to pick a specific producer who did well for a specific season, but then their next-door neighbor may have experienced the exact opposite. It was a lost decade with a few hit-or-miss productions, but never a Vintage of a Decade, as it has become known.

Then in 1982, all of a sudden, there was a once-in-a-century growing season and harvest. The weather was hot and dry, and diseases and insects—miraculously—weren't a problem. It started with a dry and sunny April. May had a few storms, but the bad weather didn't linger. The early summer months offered just the right mix of moisture with abundant sunshine. so that by harvest time in September, the grapes were bursting with flavor.

Robert Parker, still working as a lawyer at this time and moonlighting by publishing the *Wine Advocate*, was the loudest to trumpet the vintage. This became a defining moment for him as a wine advisor, as much as it was a defining moment for Bordeaux. Marvin Shanken's *Wine Spectator* wasn't far behind. Parker went so far as to recommend that people buy the wine in futures—meaning that they would pay cash for wine that wouldn't be delivered for at least another year or two.

People took his advice, and snatched up the wine. The whole event marked a turning point in wine investment. People were buying rare bottles now for investment as much as for serving or drinking. American wine tastes had finally reached maturity after the devastation of

Prohibition. An expensive bottle became the ultimate status symbol, especially on Wall Street, where brokers would split one to celebrate a big bonus or a blockbuster deal.

When I think about the 1980s and wine's emergence as a status symbol in the world of finance, I'm reminded of a story I heard once at Bern's Steakhouse in Tampa, Florida. You wouldn't know it from the restaurant's white stucco, windowless exterior, but it's probably the finest place to get a high-quality, shockingly well-priced bottle of wine with a meal.

Bern Laxer, the owner, was born in the 1920s in Manhattan, and he started the business a half century ago in a strip mall with forty seats. Over time, he bought the spaces of all the adjoining businesses and expanded to eight dining rooms, 350 seats, and one of the world's largest wine cellars. He spent decades traveling throughout the world, collecting bottles of wine, and tucking them away at the restaurant.

Bern's Steakhouse now houses more than a half-million bottles, with 6,800 unique wine labels, including Madeiras that date back to the seventeenth century. In 2010, the senior sommelier there stumbled upon a double-magnum 1947 bottle of Château Latour, priced at $30,000, and probably stored in the cellar since the 1960s. Bern died in 2002, and his son now runs the place.

The catch with buying a terrific wine for an amazing value at Bern's is that you have to drink it there. You can't buy a bottle to go. So once when I was eating dinner at the restaurant a few years ago, a bartender who had worked there practically his whole adult life told me about the time a Wall Street banker came to the restaurant with his entourage of bankers in the 1980s, and asked for "the most expensive bottle of wine in the house."

The sommelier came out and named some incredibly rare, large-format bottle from France, a Marie Jeanne (4.5 L) of 1900 or 1918 Château Margaux. The price was in the tens of thousands of dollars. The banker said, "I'll take it."

Bern came out at this point and said, "I understand you're interested in a bottle of Château Margaux."

The banker replied, "Yes, we're here to celebrate, and that's what we want."

"I'm sorry, but I can't sell you that wine," Bern said. "Right now, somewhere in the world today, someone who has less money than you has been saving for this bottle. You want this wine because it's expensive and you'd like to celebrate. This other person wants this bottle because it will be the most amazing experience of his or her life. I have plenty of other very expensive wine bottles that I'm happy to sell to you instead."

The tidal wave of cash that entered the wine industry in the 1980s changed even how old-school Bordeaux producers did business. They modernized and started employing more scientific methods to combat the effects of weather, water, and pests. They also harvested differently—waiting until the grapes ripened more deeply on the vines, to emulate the full-body taste of the popular 1982 vintage. And finally, they began to recognize the great potential in the rare wine market, so instead of using all of their grapes to produce one wine, they separated the best grapes for a premium label, and the somewhat less high-quality grapes into a second, lower-priced label.

A successful Texas businessman once told me that he became one of the early wine investors around this time because of his divorce. He didn't care about wine then, but the economy stalled and his construction partners were going out of business because no one was buying property. Banks were coming after him for loans that were on the verge of default, and his wife was trying to take half of his assets.

A couple of his buddies told him to transfer his assets into fine wine, since it was considered by the government to be a perishable item and not an investment vehicle. Therefore, it wasn't subject to asset seizure; nor was it considered property to be divided in a divorce. He double-checked with some legal advisors, then bought a whole bunch of wine. The gambit worked.

The 1990s were an equally exciting decade for wine—especially in the United States. During that decade, the industry saw a massive turnover of ownership from the post-War, post-Prohibition pioneers in California to their children. This new generation was eager to fuse modern sales and marketing techniques with the Old World art of vinification, broadening the appeal of wine even further. They also paid even more attention to the specific tastes of reviewers and adjusted their production techniques accordingly.

For instance, many wineries knew that Robert Parker liked thick, jammy red wines with high alcohol levels that were treated in oak barrels. So, many producers started making thick, jammy, high-alcohol reds and spared no expense on new French and American oak barrels, driving the price of the wines up considerably. This method of changing a wine style to meet the preferences of critics—with the hope of getting a higher score—is now cynically called

Parkerization. It began in the mid-1990s but continues today. And who blames winemakers for doing it? Scores do matter. A bottle that gets a 98, 99, or 100 sells out. It's a hot sell. Parker didn't help matters by occasionally hinting about the criteria he used for a wine to receive high marks.

A friend of mine, a Master Sommelier named Devon Broglie, once explained the subjective nature of wine ratings to me this way: Say you have an apple expert, who's paid to write about apples and talk about apples. His true passion lies with a very specific variety, though. He loves Gala apples—from the history of how they're grown, to the region of the country where their orchards are most prevalent, to who grows them. On the other hand, he hates Granny Smiths. They're naturally more acidic and too tangy for him. So when he's giving out reviews, he automatically scores Granny Smiths in the mid-80s to low 90s to start. He'll never give them more than 92 points, because he doesn't think their taste and profile will ever be deserving of it. With Galas, though, he starts at a baseline of 92, because he likes them so much better. However, the rest of the apple-eating public doesn't know this though. They automatically just believe what the apple expert says and assume that personal taste has very little to do with the scores. Before you know it, the price of Galas rise, and people gravitate toward them over

Granny Smiths. The apple orchards, to meet the demand and gain higher scores, start growing more Galas. This is like what happened with the Parkerization of wine in the 1980s.

In Europe, the 1990s started out bleakly, with several subpar vintages—while Robert Parker lauded the wines coming out of Napa. Bordeaux saw much-improved conditions in 1994, and then 1995 was considered pretty close to perfection. This vintage is considered a "sleeper" because the bottles from that year are still asleep, still closed—they're not yet in their prime drinking window. It is also not quite as widely heralded as 1982, despite the quality. The next four years were above average vintages in France, with 1990 and 1995 being superior above the rest, and 1996 not trailing too far behind.

The 2000s started with a historically fantastic year in France and a quiet one in California. One of the most pivotal events of the decade for wine attitudes in the United States actually came at the box office with the 2004 release of the movie *Sideways*.

In the film, the main character Miles and his engaged friend Jack escape to California wine country for one final buddy-bonding weekend. Miles, a wine aficionado, is obsessed with Pinot Noir and hates Merlot. His most famous line in the movie comes when he's about to go on a blind date set up by Jack. "If anyone orders Merlot," he says, "I'm leaving. I am not drinking any fucking Merlot."

After *Sideways*, Merlot sales tanked and prices fell. They've never recovered. Meanwhile, the opposite happened with Pinot Noir, particularly from Santa Barbara. Its sales went through the roof, and prices have been climbing ever since. Ironically, the wine the character Miles kept in his closet and coveted the most, a 1961 Cheval Blanc, which he ended up drinking from a paper bag while eating a burger at a fast-food restaurant, is mostly Merlot. In fact, some of the world's top wines are made from Merlot grapes, like the Petrus, Château Lafleur, Le Pin, or Château Vieux Certan, all of which come from Pomerol, a subappellation from the Right Bank of Bordeaux that focuses primarily on Merlot as the single or primary base of the wine. These wines are very expensive and coveted by collectors and the wine trade.

Another amazing vintage came to France in 2005. It was pretty close to perfect. As was 2009. All the while, a new phenomenon arose on the other side of the planet: the Asian awakening to wine, led by China. It hit the industry like a Mack truck.

Prior to 2000, the only people in Asia who drank wine from grapes (as opposed to rice wine) were the socioeconomic elites, and mostly in Japan. But around 2003, fine wine came into vogue with young professionals and business executives. Red holds a very important symbolic meaning in Chinese culture as the color of power, good luck, and wealth. People in Asia have begun to regard wine as the embodiment of these three traits.

As a result, wine has become extremely popular in the Far East in a short

amount of time—so much so that, in 2015, China emerged as the fifth largest consumer of red wine behind the United States, France, Italy, Germany, and the UK. Consequently, the demand and value of rare French wine shot upward, which was good news for investors, but not-so-good news for aficionados.

In particular, the price of Burgundy wine rose exponentially, owing in part to the fact that it's produced from such a small geographical area and by such traditionally minded winemakers. There's just a very small limit to how much wine they can produce, and there's no way for them to boost volume without bringing in grapes from another region, which would violate government standards and would cause the producers to lose their Premier Cru or Grand Cru, reducing the value of their wine into the Vin de Pays category, which is a nice way of saying "cheap wine."

Other outside factors affected the price of wine in the 2000s. For instance, oil prices rose, affecting manufacturing, packaging, shipping, farming, harvesting, and storage, inflating prices. So did the cost of grapes—the most expensive element to winemaking. Fortunately, the premium French wine market has stabilized in the past few years—the result of a cooling of Asian economies and dropping energy prices, to name a couple of factors. It's quite possible, though, given the fickle nature of the Asian market, that California wines could suddenly become trendy in that part of the world—given how approachable and fruitful some of them can be. Even better, most California wines don't require ten years or more to settle before reaching an optimum drinking window. This could turn the tables a bit in the years to come.

Another interesting phenomenon is the events surrounding the timing of the stock market crash in Hong Kong, a catalyst in the economic slowdown of the bustling Chinese economy. In 2015, Chinese consumers drank 7.24 million less gallons of wine than in the previous year. This phenomenon appeared after 5–8 percent year-over-year growth that suddenly curtailed due to the Shanghai stock market crash and an anti-corruption crackdown from Chinese dignitaries accepting fine wines as a gift. These "gifts" had immediate liquidity at local pawn shops and auction houses. For Americans, it would be inconceivable that these alone could cause a massive moving ship to come to a grinding halt, but it did happen. Hard liquor, whiskey, and scotch in particular saw a sharp incline, quite plausibly robbing from the collectibility of wines in the Asian market.

Meanwhile in the United States, a new trend is taking hold. Millennials are gravitating less to wines from traditional vineyards and more toward smaller boutique producers, or what are sometimes called garage wines. These younger buyers are often more attracted to an eye-catching label or an immediately gripping story about the winemaker than a history that dates back centuries. If a wine doesn't have a compelling narrative behind it, the millennial generation will tend to ignore it.

Another emergence in the industry is the use of crowd-sourced wine reviews. In many ways, I find them more accurate than traditional wine publications. For starters, you're relying on the opinions of a large cross section of people and not just the subjective tastes of one reviewer. Secondly, the reviews are updated constantly in real time. And indeed, wine itself isn't static—it's an organic compound that's constantly changing, sometimes for the better and sometimes for the worse, depending on age and storage conditions. For that reason, a review written a decade ago, or even last year, about a vintage may not be applicable now.

To use an example, I recently opened a bottle of 1998 Ridge Monte Bello, produced in the Santa Cruz Mountains of California. Its average score from ten years ago was about 89 points. But the wine I drank was solidly in the 90s. It's amazing right now. But *Wine Spectator* and *Wine Advocate* can't keep track of the way certain vintages may improve over time. They can only offer a best guess based on previous vintages with similar outcomes. Crowd-sourced sites do, though.

On CellarTracker.com, you've got people who own their own cellars and are reviewing wines all the time. With each new entry, a particular bottle's scoring average shifts. Reviews are constantly updated for even some of the most obscure wines. There's no way a traditional publication could keep up, or even compare.

Look at it this way: As a consumer, which review would you rather depend upon if you're walking into your cellar to pair a Pinot Noir with the pheasant you're having for dinner? A *Wine Advocate* review from 1997, or the write-up of someone who opened the very same bottle you're considering two hours ago?

There are definitely still consumers who are 100-percent driven by the traditional reviews. They'll have parties and say, "Bring only a bottle of 95 rating or higher, or don't come at all." But this type of attitude is fading, and people are better realizing the subjectivity of scoring, thanks to the amount of content now available online. The information age has also given millennials a better handle on market prices, so they're savvier about what they buy.

In the end, however, the true value of a wine comes down to a very simple set of criteria that never really changes. First is the land—its history, and what has been grown successfully there. Next is the weather: Was it sunny during that vintage? Or cloudy and rainy? Third is the harvest. Was there an abundant one, or was it uninspiring? How much wine was produced? Fifth is the winemaker. If the brand has been around a long time, you can judge them by their past vintages. If they're up-and-coming, it's good to know who the winemaker studied under and where.

THE OLD-WORLD
WINE BUSINESS

The first time I bought wine directly from producers in France was in 2005, for my company called Personal Wine (www.personalwine.com). A customer called me and requested a higher-quality wine than what I offered at that time. I made a few phone calls through friends and contacts, and found a négociant who represented a château in Haut-Medoc, in the Bordeaux region of the southwestern part of France. He was willing to sell me twenty-five cases with permission to apply custom labels, and I, in turn, provided it to my customer for $150 a bottle.

A négociant is a merchant or wholesaler who buys, sells, and sometimes bottles wine from other growers and winemakers. Until a couple of decades ago, they were the brick wall that stood between vineyard owners in France and the consumer. The setup has changed slightly thanks to direct sales on the Internet, but remains largely in existence today with regard to Bordeaux, Burgundy, and Rhone producers.

Today, the Champagne region is chalk full of traditional négociant producers who buy grapes from local farmers within the Champagne AOC (Appellation d'Origine Côntrollée). This area includes a few very famous champagne houses, including one with a famous yellow label and another with a champagne named after a famous Benedictine monk who pioneered many of the modern-day techniques used to make champagne.

The most expensive white wine in the world is Le Montrachet. This Burgundy white wine is comprised of 100 percent Chardonnay, and it is farmed by several parcel owners of the famed vineyard. One specific producer, Thenard, barrels and sells his own Le Montrachet. In addition, he sells off his Le Montrachet (in either grapes or barrels) to other producers, who then either bottle the wine directly or modify the wines to their style before bottling.

In Bordeaux, prior to the 1960s, many of the châteaus farmed their lands, produced wine in barrels, and then sold the barrels to bottlers, mostly UK retailers. This changed in the early to mid-1960s as many of the châteaus decided to begin producing wines and bottling them themselves, which is why you will see on bottles the phrase "*mis en bouteille au château*," which simply means "put into the bottle at the château [estate]."

Négociants will represent larger estates as selling agents, and actually buy finished wine in bulk from smaller winemakers, which they either blend with other wines or even bottle under their own name. Small, family-owned vineyards are often too small to affordably make wine themselves, so négociants will purchase their crops directly.

For me, the purchase of those twenty-five cases of Bordeaux was an eye-opener. I didn't realize there was any demand for high-end personalized wine until then. My impression was that, in this market, the buyers didn't care tremendously about quality. But I was wrong. I called around to clients, started doing some research, and quickly discovered this whole untapped market in the personalized wine business. This was my introduction to the fine and rare wine market.

My second experience with the French market came a short time later. One of my suppliers told me he had a remarkable opportunity to buy twenty or thirty six-packs of Grand Cru Burgundy at a distressed price. "We just need to move it," he told me. "The wine's sitting in our warehouse under temperature control, and we own it. It's an extremely good deal."

I knew very little about the wine, besides the fact that it had a $100 price tag and it was being made available to me by an incredibly trustworthy distributor at $20 a bottle. This wasn't for my personalized business, and I wasn't yet selling fine or rare wine in any quantities. Sometimes when an opportunity like this arises, you need to move instantly or it'll disappear—and this was one of those times. So I pulled the trigger. When I received the shipment, I researched the bottles and found out I had bought amazingly fine wine.

These two experiences basically were my first in the rare wine business in any large-scale way. It's kind of funny: Probably 99.9 percent of people in the industry enter it from the top end. They have an encyclopedic knowledge of vintages and regions and are—to put it bluntly—wine snobs. Yet I entered it from the opposite end. I was an amateur wine lover with very little historical context at my disposal, selling less expensive personalized products, until I realized that there was a world of rare and fine wine open to me.

The more experienced in the wine business I became, the better I began to see patterns and opportunities available to me. For instance, when I went to France one holiday with my family, I noticed that if I was in Bordeaux, the price of a specific bottle of Bordeaux was higher than if I bought it in Burgundy. The inverse was true as well. A specific bottle of Burgundy was more expensive in Burgundy than in Bordeaux.

This little lesson taught me that you shouldn't necessarily go directly to the source region where a wine is made to buy it—whether you're talking about a single bottle or on a larger scale. Instead, the byzantine and sometimes centuries-old laws that rule the industry, not to mention the exchange rates and other factors, make getting wine elsewhere less expensive. I'm not just referring to France, either. A lot of Argentine wines cost less in the United States than you can actually buy them for in Argentina.

These types of complexities and contradictions in the business scare off a lot of entrepreneurs. Wine is built on tradition and relationships that can stretch back many generations—among the growers, winemakers, négociants, distributors, and retailers. It's not a system that's optimized for the consumer, or a businessperson from the outside like me.

In France, a winery will partner with two or three négociants who sell all of their wine. The négociants will generally sit on the wine until reviewers score it, and from there the retail price—and demand—is set. If the product is going to the United States, it will be sent to an importer, who ships it overseas and to a specific state—since all states have different liquor laws—where a distributor receives it. Finally, the distributor delivers it to a retailer, who then resells it to consumers. Although the three-tier system has been in place since Prohibition, it's an inefficient, cost-prohibitive oligopoly built upon a tight-knit network of a small number of people.

The inefficiency of the system is fiercely protected because everyone in the custody chain wants to get a slice of the action, to keep making a living. The closer you get to buying wine from the source, the less expensive it's going to be, but the more you're upsetting the traditional ways. And winemakers are reluctant to let in outsiders, anyway, or to jump past links in the custody chain, because they don't like to wander too far into the unknown. There is evidence that this antiquated system, which is ripe for disruption, may change.

In 2012, Château Latour announced the end of releasing wines via the traditional futures system. Instead the château would release wines closer to when the wines are ready to be released and would commence château-direct purchasing. A few other châteaus from Bordeaux have since followed this path.

Besides, the producers know that they need strong relationships with importers and distributors to get placements with the most popular fine wine markets and best steakhouses and, in turn, access to the right customers. Ironically, the more a bottle changes hands before reaching the consumer, the worse it is for the integrity of the wine because of vibration, movement, and less control over storage conditions. Yet this circuitous distribution method lives on. Wine is the most fragile of all alcoholic beverages. In an ideal situation, it would be kept in controlled conditions at all times, passed between the fewest people possible.

The wine networks in France are so tight-knit that even when wineries are sold, it's usually to another winery owner. Outsiders can only crack through by paying a high premium. The producers of rare, collectible wines almost never sell, because their châteaus are entrenched within a family and follow a lineage. Winery owners wear their titles like royalty—especially one family in particular: the Rothschilds.

The Rothschilds are one of the wealthiest families in the world, descendants of wealthy German bankers. Over the last several centuries, their dynasty has spread throughout Europe, into Austria, England, Italy, and France. In the nineteenth century, at various times, the family's London bank actually propped up the British government on a couple of occasions. The French side of the Rothschilds entrenched themselves in mining and railroads, and they also became known as the first family of wine. They entered the winemaking industry in 1853, when Nathaniel Rothschild bought Château Brane Mouton and renamed it Château Mouton Rothschild. About fifteen years later, his uncle James Mayer de Rothschild bought a winery nearby and called it Château Lafite Rothschild. The family then bought many other estates throughout France, as well as a handful in North America, South America, South Africa, and Australia. Bottles from Château Mouton Rothschild and Château Lafite Rothschild are called First Growth, or Premier Cru Classe—a classification dating back to 1855 that's only given to the finest and priciest wines produced in Bordeaux.

During the occupation of France in World War II, many of the Rothschilds fled the country because they were Jewish. German garrisons were set up inside both Château Lafite Rothschild and Château Mouton Rothschild, and the invading forces cleaned out many of the cellared wines there. Fortunately, in the Rothschilds' absence, large caches of their inventories were secretly transported to other French wineries, which hid and stored them. The surrounding château owners went so far as to build secret compartments within their wine cellars to stash Rothschild wines, to be returned after the war.

This sense of loyalty, camaraderie, and responsibility among French wine producers exists today. In Burgundy, each year after harvest and bottling, the region's estates will exchange cases of wines with each other as gifts. Every spring, they join together to hold an En Primeur, which is basically an annual gathering where select industry insiders are allowed to sample the latest vintage from the barrel. Much of the wine is then sold before it's even put in a bottle, on a futures basis. A similar event is held each year in Bordeaux.

These types of tasting gatherings are where the hype for a vintage starts. The ratings experts in attendance, from *Wine Spectator* to *Burgundy Report* and the like, even give the vintage an initial score range. Prices get established at this time, based upon these scores, along with the harvest conditions for the vintage and the background on the vineyards themselves—down to the variables in their oak barrels and the placement of their storage areas. Tradition rules in France.

The only changes in winemaking methods in Burgundy and Bordeaux have been for the better—like the use of laser optics to sort grapes, based on their quality, or advances in cork production to sharply reduce instances of spoiled wine due to Trichloroanisole (TCA), commonly referred by the layman as "corked wine."

But the use of technology much past this point isn't allowed because it would violate the ages-old rules governing wine production and classification. The penalty for not adhering to a set of standards governed by the AOC authorities can vary, but it can include forced declassification of wines, fines, and in some rare instances jail time.

Not that these En Primeurs are the only places where a wine can generate a buzz. A tremendous number of buying commitments, and expert wine reviews, are made at Vinexpo, a wine showcase event held every other year in Bordeaux that usually attracts more than fifty thousand visitors, as well as at the annual ProWein in Germany, which has similar attendance—all after tasting samples from a barrel.

The problem is that many things can happen to wine by the time it goes into a bottle. Each individual barrel possesses unique properties that can affect how a vintage tastes. Bottling it is also a disruptive process that causes unpredictable results. Revised scores for a wine after it's released to the public (and poured from a bottle) can fluctuate quite a bit, up or down, making large futures investments a gamble.

Regardless of this fact, when a barrel score comes in at the high to mid-90s, the exuberance for that product in the market is incredible. People will start declaring it a "vintage of the decade." The prices hike. Then sometimes down the line, everyone realizes that the vintage doesn't live up to the hype. If you're lucky, you can catch a wine that experiences the opposite: it's underrated in the barrel but tastes amazing out of the bottle.

This is not to diminish the work of the reviewers. They do use other data points when making their scores, beyond personal tastes. They compare the weather, and presence of pests and fungus, to that of other timeless vintages. They know the winemakers and the quality of the products they create, as well as the estate's terroir. But in reality, to me, there's no difference between a 97-point wine and a supposedly perfect 100-point one. Maybe the 100-pointer will last for fifty years or more, and that's the big difference, but I'm probably not going to be around in a half-century, so I don't really care. Even if a wine holds its value for a longer period of time, most people aren't going to hold on to a bottle for fifty years.

How the châteaus hook the distributors into committing to larger orders of wine in this tasting-from-the-barrel process is really interesting. Generally, each year a wine-maker will produce at least two or three different wines. They'll have the Grand Cru, which is made from the finest grapes and generates the most talk among reviewers and other influence makers at the En Primeurs. Then they'll create a second label that consists of wine that doesn't quite live up to elite standards or uses grapes from younger, not quite mature vines. And finally, some will produce a third-label product, which would be basically an inexpensive table wine that comes from batches or blends of grapes harvested from their vineyards that are good, but not great.

The winemakers will only make the Grand Cru—the big dog of their offerings—available to the distributors on the condition that they also order a certain number of cases of the second and third labels, which are harder to sell. For distributors, the most powerful weapon in their arsenal against retailers is their book, listing the brands and wines they carry. The more big dogs they've got, the more leverage they hold over retailers. So it's in their best interest to keep the top vineyards happy, and they agree to the arrangement.

If a distributor declines to take the second and third labels, the estate will simply move on to someone who will. But everyone wants the Grand Cru, so this almost never happens. The distributors need to make money, too, so they make a similar demand to the retailers. They'll say, "If you want us to offer you the Grand Cru from Estate X, you've also got to take these other cases off my hands."

This model trickles down to the high-end consumer. It's common for a retailer to say to a wine enthusiast, "You want a bottle of this collectible wine? Well, you also have to buy bottles of these second and third labels as well." They get away with this because the Grand Crus are so popular and hard to get. These are special customers given access to wines that are never actually even placed on the retailer's shelf.

Let's say, for instance, you're new to collecting wine and you want a bottle of Coche-Dury Corton-Charlemagne, made in the Côte de Beaune region of Burgundy. You can't just walk into a typical high-end retail store and get it. The retailer is going to say, "You'll have to wait in line. I've got a list of fifty customers who also want it, and the people at the top have been waiting to get their hands on a bottle for fifteen years. They've got the right of first refusal." When these customers' names are finally called, they're going to be more than willing to buy a few bottles of second- and third-label wines to get their prize. Meanwhile, if you want a bottle immediately, you'll have to buy it on the secondary market through a broker.

The second- and third-label wines are essential products for estates, particularly in France. They've got to produce as much wine as possible in order to maximize revenues, but with a limited amount of real estate. If a portion of the harvest is subpar—for any number of reasons—they've still got to find a way to squeeze out a profit from as many grapes as possible. There's very little margin for error. Such is the life of a business that places its fate in the cruel hands of the weather.

The only aspect of winemaking that's truly under full control of the estates is the integrity of their product. For that reason, it's something that they protect vigorously, as do their regional and national governments. Once doubt creeps into the minds of consumers about the origin and quality of a wine, its value plummets and will likely never recover. The stain of impropriety can then potentially ruin the reputation of other innocent winemakers from across the region, or even the entire country, which would have a devastating effect. Therefore, if a winemaker commits fraud by, say, blending grapes from another region into a wine, that winemaker will be subject to vigorous prosecution. High-profile criminal prosecutions have occurred recently in Italy and Burgundy over this very matter.

Regions also aggressively enforce their trademarked names. Only sparkling wine from the Champagne region in France can be called champagne. Rioja can only come from the eponymous region of north-central Spain. The same even goes for inexpensive products. Only a Portuguese fortified wine, for instance, can truly be labeled Port.

Every bottle a California estate sells is regulated and protected as well. Producers need to fill out paperwork spelling out exactly what's coming from their wineries, and how they're labeled. You can't get away with calling a wine a Howell Mountain if you bought the grapes from the Napa Valley floor. The trail of documentation simply won't let you. You'd have to declassify the wine from any specific appellation—and simply call it wine from California—before the federal government would allow you sell it.

It has taken me years to understand and master the nuances of the business, but they're necessary tasks for a wine broker. My strength is as an expert who has an advanced knowledge of wine, regions, and vintages. If I'm going to facilitate a sale between someone who owns a rare or collectible wine and an oenophile who wants to purchase it for investment or enjoyment, my depth of background on the product needs to be as great as, or greater than, theirs.

Estate Wine Brokers specializes in rare and back vintage wines for very discerning and usually avidly wine-loving customers. In nuts-and-bolts terms, we do the following:

1. Find people with allocations they don't want.
2. Find odd lots that will perform better in the broker's market than at auction.
3. Find specific wines buyers seek.
4. Match buyers with sellers.
5. Put our expertise and reputation behind ensuring that a bottle of wine is what it should be.

We also help restaurateurs and retailers elevate their wine programs, and we offer appraisals of a client's wine cellar for insurance purposes.

On a personal level, my job as a broker is to provide a high level of customer service and to offer my clients complete confidence in the investments they are making. We want to build fruitful, long-lasting relationships, so we do our homework and guarantee provenance, and we always stand by our work. We try to sell piece of mind with every transaction.

Not all brokers are created equal, and you can find plenty of fly-by-night operations that want to make a quick buck and move on. The small community of reputable brokers all know each other, though, and sometimes we even work together to find the right bottle for a specific client, because each one of us has established our own unique set of sources. Fly-by-night brokers are out of this loop.

They're also never going to look out for the client's interests the way I would.

One time I had a businessman customer who wanted to buy a bottle of Petrus Pomerol from the banner vintage, 1982. It's made of Merlot grapes—yes, Merlot!—that come from a Bordeaux estate that dates back to the early nineteenth century. This customer had just won a big settlement in court, and he wanted to celebrate with this exact bottle—immediately. He also said he wouldn't pay more than $4,000 for it, which was the going rate in the market at the time.

I found a bottle through a broker I trust and whose reputation is impeccable. After scrutinizing the labels, seals, and provenance, I bought it for barely below my client's ceiling price, and I had it shipped overnight to him in Las Vegas (where else was he going to celebrate?). I took a loss in the deal, considering the insurance, shipping costs, transaction fees, time spent, and overhead. But the client and I had shared a long-standing, profitable partnership, and I wanted to come through for him.

Not all of my stories have happy endings, of course. Sometimes I find myself in the position of walking away from deals that don't make financial sense—either for the buyer, for the seller, or for me. Occasionally I have to turn down the opportunity to buy caches of rare wine that give me doubts about their condition or authenticity. Just this year I flew to New York City to inspect three bottles of 1945 Château Mouton Rothschild. This is the most faked wine on the planet. This bottle, if real and in good shape from a solid source, would command a price as high as $12,000 to $15,000 per bottle.

Upon arrival and inspection of the bottles, I noticed inconsistencies in the glass, labels, and font used in the serial numbers. Upon cutting the capsule to see what was written on the cork, I noticed that someone had taken a bottle of 1955 Mouton Rothschild and relabeled it as 1945 Mouton Rothschild. The sad part about this is that the 1955 Mouton Rothschild is also an outstanding wine, but because the bottle had been compromised, I couldn't buy it or sell it in good conscience. I blew $2,000 getting to New York City in a snowstorm, lost my bags at the airport, had to buy new clothes, and lost the wine deal, which was the sole intent of the trip.

Another unfortunate story is about when, in the middle of August in the hot Texas summer, a man appeared at my office, unsolicited, with thirty cases of wine sitting in the bed of a truck. He said, "My father-in-law passed away, and he had this wine collection. Can you appraise it all for me?"

Under the circumstances, I was reluctant to do it, but at the same time I was curious—and he was desperate. I told him to bring them in, and I'd take a look. The first bottle I pulled from the cases was a 1990 Domaine de la Romanee-Conti La Tache Grand Cru, made from Pinot Noir grapes by a vineyard in Burgundy that was established by monks in the early 1600s. The next bottle was a 1982 Château Margaux, which is one of the five First Growths of Bordeaux and comes from an estate established in the twelfth century. My first thought was, *Okay, this is a significant collection.*

I asked the man where the wine was stored. He replied that it was in his father-in-law's garage in a wine cooler that had been turned off since June. I was devastated—not so much for the lost opportunity, but for the lost art that these bottles represented. It was as if someone had spilled paint thinner on a Rembrandt. The wine was no good to me, much less to a future buyer. After being stored in the hot Texas summer conditions, it was vinegar. I gave the man my assessment, and he was visibly upset.

But he refused to listen and pressed for a valuation—any valuation. He asked what the collection would be worth in prime condition. I told him I wouldn't furnish any kind of number, and I warned him against trying to take the cases to auction. I told him the wine was not sellable, even for ten cents on the dollar. It was barely collectible for the value of the empty bottle and label. I don't tell people where to dump wine, simply because I would never want to be on the receiving end of a similar transaction. I also try to dissuade people from selling empty bottles of highly collectible wine because I don't want the bottles falling into the hands of counterfeiters.

He pressed on, saying he'd pay me just to take inventory of the cases, so he could know what he had. I refused again. I didn't want my name attached to this wine, under any circumstances. He walked out the door, and lo and behold, two weeks later I saw a message he posted on a Wine Spectator online forum saying that he was taking the bottles to auction on WineBid.com but was willing to sell them privately if possible, to avoid paying fees. From the post, it was clear that he wasn't disclosing the condition of the wines.

I called him and said, "I told you before, you can't sell that wine." To him, this was just business. But to me, wine is my livelihood and passion, and if this type of shady deal goes through, it could—in some small but meaningful way—affect the entire fine wine community, including my colleagues, clients, and me.

BUYING, DRINKING, AND SELLING WHAT'S LEFT

Ernest Hemingway once wrote, "Wine is one of the most civilized things in the world, and one of the most natural things that has been brought to the greatest perfection. It offers a greater range for enjoyment and appreciation than, possibly, any other purely sensory thing."

I agree completely, which is why I'm a wine broker and not a stockbroker. I'm lucky enough to combine my business with my personal passion. Most people in the wine business share this feeling. But as with stocks and bonds, the wine business is still a bottom-line endeavor, and you as an investor are better served when you have a keen understanding of where you're putting your money—even when you're working with a broker.

My recommendation to all new investors is to study the top wines from France and the United States first. These two countries form the backbone of the industry, and they're where the most acclaimed and valuable wines predominantly come from. Understanding the differences and similarities between French and American winemaking techniques, typical weather patterns, grape varietals, and terroir will enable you to appreciate the subtleties between bottles and vintages and to truly see why a twenty-five-ounce bottle of aged, fermented grape juice can sometimes be considered to be worth more money than a Ferrari.

Once you've got the basics down on the rare wine market, you can expand your knowledge to better include what interests you—from vintages produced in other countries, to the inner workings of industry trends and consumer behavior. Of course, your research would never be complete without sampling lots and lots of wine along the way, preferably by attending wine dinners and joining wine tours with other aficionados.

When I'm working with new customers, my first goal is to figure out their taste profile. I or someone from my company will ask them a series of questions to discern their preferences, and then eventually make recommendations for building up a cellar based on those criteria. Personal taste is important to discern because most people aren't exclusively buying wine as an investment. Instead, they're cracking open some of the bottles over time. In an ideal situation, my clients are using the profits from their investments to fund their expensive tastes in rare wine. I'm always happy when a customer is essentially drinking for half-price or, better yet, for free.

On the flip side, there are definitely people who buy rare and collectible wine solely to drink. They're simpler customers to satisfy, because we have a good idea of what they want and what their budgets are, and we can cater to those specific criteria. The type of customer I usually see, though, is the person who buys nine bottles and will end up drinking three and holding on to or selling the other six.

Once clients buy a bottle, we always ensure that they've secured a way to protect the investment. Do they have their own climate- and humidity-controlled wine cellar? Or have they rented a unit in a commercial wine storage facility? They can't just store the wine in a closet or in a basement. There is also the matter of maintaining an inventory of their holdings, once they've built up a large collection. We offer to track their investments in our database system, and we provide a general appraisal of their inventory each year. This arrangement also allows us to better connect buyers and sellers.

The biggest challenge to wine investing is the emotional attachment you, as a collector, can make with a rare bottle. Frankly, it can be hard to sell, just as it would be difficult to part with a beautiful heirloom painting hanging in your living room. If you'd rather hold on to it, that's fine. We respect that. But we need to establish what your wishes are, up front, because we can't offer a bottle for sale unless you're absolutely ready to make a move.

For that reason, at the beginning of our relationship with clients, we also provide a consultation that will give us a baseline idea of what their buying and—eventually— selling preferences are. Do you want to get into the wine market solely for investment purposes? Are you planning on amassing a collection to fill your personal wine cellar? A little of both? Or maybe you simply want to buy a few rare bottles as a one-time deal, or as a gift to a friend.

Once we get a feel for the client's needs, the search for bottles begins. For me, the three most important criteria for considering a rare wine to buy are its tradition, the length of time it has been aged, and the winemakers. I'd rather steer people to a blue-chip bottle that has a significant pedigree than chase the trends with some catchy label that isn't guaranteed to have longevity. I've found that the wines produced by the people who have been in business for decades, or even centuries, invariably maintain better price integrity and generate more profit for my clients in the long-term than ones that come from relatively nowhere to become the rage.

Another facet of wine investing I avoid, as I've mentioned earlier, is the volatile futures market. It seems ridiculous to me that someone would speculatively buy a vintage based on its barrel score, one or two years before it's even released. The system works great for the winemakers, of course, because it helps them cover the production costs and see revenues much more quickly. Futures aren't as much of a winning proposition for a buyer, though. As I've mentioned, wine is an organic compound that is constantly changing, and if a vintage doesn't continue on an upward trajectory to excellence, the investor is out of luck. The increased volatility of prices due to trends in Asia has hurt futures in recent years as well. Consumer tastes in that part of the world have a tendency to change with breathtaking speed, sending the market on short-term roller-coaster rides. The recent boom-and-bust cycles of Asian economies have further compounded matters.

For instance, Bordeaux was extremely popular among the elites in China about a decade ago. It had turned into a status symbol in a culture that is becoming obsessed with conspicuous consumption. People there wanted to be seen in a restaurant with a high-priced Bordeaux sitting at the table, label facing toward the crowd.

In turn, the value of some rare bottles grew as much as 100 percent annually. Then around 2010, just as suddenly as Bordeaux had come into vogue, the spigot turned off and demand died. Part of the change could be attributed to fashion tastes, which shifted on a dime toward Burgundies. Also at this time, though, the Chinese premier announced a massive austerity drive that clamped down on the use of public funds by high-ranking government officials for personal lifestyle expenses. So the money was diverted to other markets.

People in Asia put the brakes on Bordeaux so quickly and completely that millions of dollars of orders were canceled or defaulted upon. Some shipments to China were even sent back to the wholesalers in France, who in turn sent everything back to the wineries. The price bubble burst, and the producers were left trying to find a way to unload their inventories.

There's a famous story about one négociant named Philippe Papillon, who was considered the top Asia specialist in France at the time. Shortly before the market collapsed, he had transferred the title of around $10 million worth of wine to a consortium in China, but the buyer defaulted and the shipment never left Bordeaux. He sued to regain ownership and won. It was the first time a négociant had ever repossessed wine from a buyer. Imagine if you had invested a large sum of money in Bordeaux futures at this time.

Just as risky as futures investments are purchases made at auction. You can definitely get some great deals, but you're never quite guaranteed of what you're buying—or of what price you're going to get if you're selling. I will say that I do have tremendous respect for a very short list of auction houses—especially, Hart Davis Hart. Their intense inspection process and commitment to accurately listing conditions and disclosures is the most thorough I have seen to date.

In contrast to this, I steer my clients toward a longer-term, less speculative approach to the market, one that is less prone to the ups and downs of shifting trends and tastes. In turn, my clients have reaped better and more consistently stable returns. With my business, transactions are conducted more discreetly, faster, and with more security and price certainty. The chain of custody is never under question or broken either. If you sell a bottle at auction, on the other hand, you have to ship the product to the auction house for inspection, photography, and eventually sale. On top of that, there's a payout period that delays the transaction for ninety days or more after the winning bid is made. Most concerning, as a buyer at auction, is that you're not always privy to the provenance of a wine, because half the time the sellers don't attach their names to the bottle, which can leave you more vulnerable to exposure.

With my business, you'll generally know how much you're going to make or spend on a bottle of wine before the transaction. I'll give you a specific price—whether you're buying or selling. Auction houses only provide a range of possible prices, from low to high, and you don't know how a bottle will perform on a given day.

There are other distinctive advantages a broker offers. Let's say there's a specific bottle you really want that's included in a lot you're considering that's being sold for $10,000 or $15,000. You'd be willing to overpay for that bottle if you're getting a great deal on two or three other bottles included in the parcels. The transaction becomes more about overall numbers than specific items, and at the end of the day, you're going to be buying a cellar's worth of wine at a discount, including the coveted bottle. If you and the broker turn around and sell some of those bargain bottles for a profit, your financial benefit increases even more. You don't have this type of flexibility when you're buying wines at auction.

Finally, and maybe most importantly, my job as a broker is to provide personal service to each of my clients. I'm their detective, finding them a specific vintage that they want to buy, or seeking the right buyer for wine they want to sell. I strive to understand them and exactly what their needs are. Auction houses are great at what they do, but they're not geared toward creating a personalized experience.

I always try to be a good listener. There are a lot of egos in the wine business because of the art factor, but ultimately you can learn a lot about people just by keeping an open mind, and not necessarily telling them what they should be doing, or trying to convince them to go in a specific direction.

Of course, not all brokers are created equal. Before you do business with one, visit their physical location first to see how long they've been around, and how permanent their operation seems. You want to find someone who has tenure, who knows the business well and can effectively handle transactions of all kinds, large and small. Be sure they're licensed, and ask for references. The broker should be able to tell you about a time when something bad happened and how he or she fixed the situation. Treat the visit like you're conducting a job interview, because essentially you are.

You're hiring someone whom you need to be able to trust to handle large sums of your money and who will understand your needs. You don't want a broker who is buying and selling feverishly just to make commissions, without logic. The smart brokers realize that happy customers turn into referrals, and word-of-mouth marketing is essential in the wine business, as it is in any segment of the investment world. The network of contacts I've created through referrals stretches around the world.

A good broker should also work well with people of all backgrounds, cultures, and countries. My personal interactions are what make me so excited to come to the office every morning. I've met some amazing people and uncovered incredible treasures that have come from the most unlikely places and circumstances.

Domestically, hidden gems can arise from anywhere. One day I might stumble across a collection abandoned by wine sellers who haven't paid their bills. Or I might be led to a cellar inherited by people not interested in wine. Or I'll get a call from a restaurant that has gone out of business or is looking for cash, or an estate sale, or a wine fund looking to divest. There's also the occasional divorce.

My most rewarding moment as a broker comes when I'm able to use my detective skills and experience to connect someone with that one special bottle that will create a lifetime memory. Once I was contacted by a prominent couple in Houston whose two daughters were both getting married in a joint ceremony. One of the girls was born in 1986, and the other in 1988. The girls' father wanted to get a large-format bottle, at least twelve liters, from each of those two vintages, so he could pop each bottle open at the wedding and share it with family and friends.

I explained to him that the total cost would be in excess of $10,000, because few estates in modern times put rare wines in bottles larger than six liters, and those that do are on the truly high end, because they're usually only produced on request for amazing customers. Plus, the vintages had to fall within the proper drinking window. He was unfazed, though, and said, "Go find them." This was two months before the wedding.

I immediately put the word out to my network of clients and contacts, and I pounded the pavement for leads. It took me nearly all of the sixty days to strike gold. But as the wedding approached, one of my sources at a winery reached out. He happened to have, in his own collection, two bottles that met my requirements, and he was willing to sell. The 1986 was a Cabernet Sauvignon from Silver

Oak Winery in Napa, and the 1988 was a Bordeaux from the nearly two-centuries-old Château Cheval Blanc in Bordeaux. I knew the provenance was good, and I was able to produce the bottles to my clients just under the wire.

I'm told that when my client popped the corks at the ceremony, the moment was spectacular. The wine was still youthful and drinking well, and the experience of sharing those large-format bottles from the birth years of his children was over-the-top for him. I feel pretty great about the deal, too, knowing that I made two hundred wedding guests very happy, and gave a family a moment to savor for the rest of their lives.

To me, experiences like this really epitomize why I sell wine. I'm not interested in just making lots of money from buying one item and then turning that transaction around to buy something else with the intent of making more money. Certainly, generating a profit is nice—and important—for my clients and me, but I find equal satisfaction in the unique, emotional element of when someone opens a bottle of wine for an important, special occasion to appreciate the artwork housed within it.

Not long after the wedding, this same customer called me looking to buy several bottles of a very specific kind of wine from a very specific producer for another important occasion. It happened that I knew someone who had collected the wine. But I said to him, "Well, let's wait a minute. How about you buy one bottle and try it. If it's good, then you can buy the other ones. That way you're not stuck buying something that you don't like"

He agreed, so I purchased one bottle of the wine, we opened it up, and it just wasn't right for him. I avoided a transaction that could have left a negative impression. In an inverse way, this moment was also a rewarding one for me, even though I didn't make any money, because I protected the interest of my client and kept him happy.

Though every search for a bottle is different, I use the same general approach each time. My initial step is to search the existing database of wines held in the cellars that my company helps manage for clients. We've put eyes on those bottles, we know the history of the wine, and so we have greater confidence in what we've got.

If we don't have a specific bottle within our network, we'll reach out to other brokers whom we trust. If we strike out there, I'll call some of the auction houses where I have personal relationships, and ask them if that bottle is coming up for sale. If there's still no luck, I'll search the retailer database to see who has what products and what prices, and then I'll look at the conditions of the wine, the fill levels, and the clarity. I have other proprietary detective methods for searching for a specific bottle as well. Throughout the process, I provide regular status reports to clients to keep them constantly updated on our progress.

I love the thrill of the hunt for a bottle, and how the market landscape changes on a daily basis. Even the financial status of my clients is a variable that needs to be taken into account. Right now, for instance, it's very difficult to sell fine wines to oil and gas clients, given the drop in energy prices.

What makes me a great hunter, and seller, is my competitive spirit. I like to win, while maintaining high integrity. To this end, I've built extensive resources and a beautiful company inside and out. We have a physical location that is insured and licensed, and we have amazing, talented people who are always going to be looking out for the client.

My relationships within the business are time-tested. They're my friends as much as my colleagues. During a hunt, they might break off a crumb of information for me. Those crumbs turn into morsels when combined with information from other people, and those morsels can turn into a loaf of bread.

Another important service that I—and most reputable brokers—provide is the comprehensive valuation of wine collections. This work is performed for a fee. My company digs into the provenance, history, and past storage conditions of each wine to determine its unique market value. We also include a physical inspection conducted by either my lead man or me. Few other companies take their appraisals to this level of detail.

Because deals can take place so quickly in the wine industry, I try to respond almost immediately to a call from someone who is interested in selling all or parts of his or her collection. Timing is everything. If I can handle a deal in forty-eight hours that would take most other companies ten days to two weeks to complete, I'm instantly at an advantage.

This means that sometimes I'm buying a plane ticket and heading to the airport as soon as I get off the phone. I'll go anywhere in the country to perform an appraisal, at any time. I'll move so fast that I won't have time to pack my clothes, and on occasion I'll find myself going to Target wherever I land to buy toothpaste and underwear. If I'm working with a seller who is presenting an incredible opportunity, and I don't have a buyer instantly lined up, I'll occasionally take the risk and buy the inventory myself, with the intent of selling it down the line.

A broker's fees come from a percentage of a successful transaction, as in real estate. About 50 percent of the time, I'm working opposite another broker—either on the buying or selling side—in which case the fee is split. I don't mind split-fee transactions, because they incentivize relationships with other brokers and expand my network of contacts. When the sale of, say, $100,000 worth of investments is taking place, the buyer and seller usually feel more comfortable if there isn't one single person facilitating the entire deal. They'll each want an expert sitting in their corner, specifically looking out for their best interests, which is perfectly sensible.

As part of our services, my company employs lawyers who will draw up a contract for the transaction. Legal considerations should always be taken into account, covering how the money will change hands; what the chain of custody, shipping, and storage will be; what guarantees on the sale will be made; and the buyer's right to inspect a bottle upon receipt to ensure its authenticity and condition. Lawyers are also necessary to ensure that state liquor laws are correctly followed during the sale and delivery of the wine.

In most cases, the transaction is pretty straightforward in the eyes of the law because the broker isn't an importer or distributor; he's simply a third-party intermediary, providing the specific service of authentication, evaluation, and price between a buyer and a seller. Typically, buyers are simply importing the wine for their own personal collection, which most states allow without too much regulation.

My role as broker is to provide advice and counsel on ways to maximize your investments—as in avoiding futures, and buying and selling the right bottles at the right times. There are occasions when clients want to hold on to a wine at a time when I've detected a temporary spike in the market, due to a variety of factors, from the opening of a vintage's drink window to a sudden shift in international tastes and trends. It's my role at that moment to tell them, "You know, your Burgundy is at peak market value right now. It's never been higher. If you're interested in selling, you could probably do it right now and buy it back in five years for cheaper than what you originally bought it for." Sometimes clients follow my advice, and sometimes they decide to keep it in their cellar a little longer. Sometimes they'll even tell me that they've decided to drink it themselves.

The return on investment for someone who's shrewd and patient can be extremely impressive. Someone in the 1980s who bought high-end Bordeaux at a release price of about $35 per bottle could sell it today for roughly $1,000 on average. Château Lafite Rothschild, which is an outlier, would sell today for north of $3,000 per bottle. People who bought 2000 Bordeaux from Costco for about $150

FAMED WINE FRAUDS

Sadly enough, all rare wine buyers today are at risk for fraud. It's the role of a skilled broker to investigate the provenance and authenticity of any bottles you're considering for purchase, in order to protect you and your money. There are two famous instances of elaborate wine fraud that are so incredible they're almost impossible to believe. One involved four bottles of 1787 Bordeaux that were supposedly owned by Thomas Jefferson, and another centered on an Indonesian expat named Rudy Kurniawan.

In the first instance, American billionaire Bill Koch spent roughly $500,000 in the late 1980s on four bottles of wine: a 1787 Branne Mouton, a 1784 Branne Mouton, a 1784 Lafitte, and a 1787 Lafitte. They all had supposedly been found a decade earlier in a bricked-up cellar in Paris, and were believed to be from a collection owned by Thomas Jefferson. The engravings etched onto the glass were evaluated by experts and considered authentic, and other wines from the Jefferson cache had been tasted and pronounced real—and excellent.

Nearly two decades after the transaction, Koch's staff decided to track down the provenance of the bottles and discovered them to be fakes. Jefferson experts from Monticello said they didn't believe the story to be credible, and forensic scientists said the etchings on the glass were made by power tools. Through further investigation, it turned out that the bottles had all originated from a German wine collector named Hardy Rodenstock, who made several other too-good-to-believe finds. To this day he's fighting multiple court cases filed against him for allegedly selling fake wines.

The second famous fraud case, involving Rudy Kurniawan, is even more surprising. In 2012, federal agents raided his home in Beverly Hills, California, and found bottles soaking in a sink, as well as a machine for recorking and thousands of fake labels for expensive wines that he had printed. At that time, he was an incredibly well-known name in wine circles, and he had been flooding the auction markets with an incredible number of rare vintages, worth tens of millions of dollars.

His whole scheme originally began to fall apart at an auction in 2008, when he put up for sale more than 250 bottles of rare Burgundy from three of the world's top producers, including bottles of Domaine Ponsot Grand Cru supposedly dating back to 1929. During the event, the owner of Ponsot appeared and informed the auctioneer that his estate didn't start producing the Grand Cru until 1934. Kurniawan responded to the controversy by implying that his supplier had duped him. "We try our best to get it right, but it's Burgundy and sometimes shit happens," he told *Wine Spectator*.

But the hunt was on by people in industry circles to get to the truth. Koch, while still investigating the Jefferson wine, also discovered that 211 bottles in his cellar supplied by Kurniawan were suspicious and likely fakes. The FBI got involved, and after Kurniawan's arrest, he was indicted on mail and wire fraud. Kurniawan was sentenced in 2013 to ten years in prison. I would say the lesson here is simple: if you screw rich people, then you're going to get really screwed back. An uberwealthy wine collector will actually spend ten times the amount of money he paid for the original fraudulent transaction on a lawsuit to prove a point.

on release could sell it for $1,500 to $2,000 now. With 2000 Mouton, the release price was also about $150, and they currently go for almost $1,500 apiece on the auction markets. On average, I'd say if people are investing in wine from multiple regions, they could realize returns of eight to 10 percent annually, if they wait a decade and they're shrewd.

The drinkability window always plays an important factor in value, of course. For Napa, it can be three to five years after release, for Bordeaux about ten years, and for Burgundy anywhere from five years to a decade. As the window opens, and people begin popping corks and reviewers start to score the wine once again, the hype filters into the mainstream media and grabs the public's attention. At the same time, sommeliers are tasting the wine, talking about it, and recommending the wine on the floor of restaurants. This domino effect brings the wine back to life, and invigorates its value in the process.

Great bottles typically have tremendous longevity, but wines can go dormant in the eyes of the public after the release phase. Some people will sell it off during this sleeping period—usually due to some financial difficulties rather than for profit reasons—to convert the wine to cash, creating an ideal buying opportunity, because the demand is usually low at this time. In the life of a typical Burgundy,

Bordeaux, or Napa wine, you'll probably have three peak periods when the window opens and the buzz spikes.

Just as you're looking for bargains when a wine is dormant, you never want to buy a bottle during its peak. If you're reading about it in *Wine Spectator*, you're probably too late. You need to stay on the leading end, keeping an eye on emerging winemakers and what the market portends in the next year or two for the traditional producers. Stay in the know. Join tasting groups and tours for aficionados. Find people who have played in the wine game before, and pick their brain to learn their best strategies. Subscribe to online forums like Wine Berserkers (www.wineberserkers.com/forum) to track the trends and see what hot topics are being discussed.

Some of the smartest, and friendliest, wine experts you'll find are the sommeliers. Find the best steakhouse within a two-hour drive, and reserve a table. When you're there, pick the sommelier's brain, and ask where to find the best local places to taste wine and find other collectors. Another great way to network and learn is to attend conferences like the Miami Wine Fair, the New York Wine Expo, and the Texas Sommeliers Conference (TEXSOM). At these events, you'll see top wine collectors sitting together, sharing experiences, discussing their perceptions of the market, and—most importantly—sharing bottles of great wine together.

As part of the learning process, you'll want to pay as much attention to who the predominant buyers will be in the near horizon and far in the future. Accurately predicting what will be in demand, and with whom, is ultimately essential to investing success. For instance, did you know that China officially became one of the world's largest consumers of red wines? They buy 155 million cases a year, which puts them ahead of France. Savvy investors will tell you that consumers there have less of an understanding of wine because of the lack of tradition and experts in the field. So they tend to gravitate toward high-alcohol, conspicuously high-status wines with well-known labels.

Millennials in the United States, born between 1980 and 2000, on the other hand, are gravitating in a completely different direction. For them, tradition means little. They're more interested in an interestingly designed label and in finding a young, up-and-coming entrepreneurial craft winemaker with an interesting story. An estate that has been making wine the same way for five centuries seems stale, musty, and not as immediate to them.

You may not think that millennials have tremendous buying power, but their impact on the market is growing tremendously and will affect your long-term investments. They already outnumber baby boomers as a slice of the American population, according to the most recent census, by 8 million. So, if you're investing in wine that you don't want to sell for another ten to fifteen years, millennials are going to be your main buyers by that time. They'll have worked their way to the top of the ladder to the higher-paying jobs by then and will be the people with disposable incomes to spend. To get a handle on their way of thinking, you'll need to talk to younger people in the wine industries, such as aspiring sommeliers studying for their certification exams, and pick their brains.

This is not to say that traditional winemakers will ever truly lose their place in the market. Trends come and go, but consistent quality will always have a seat at the bar. The question is whether the old estates are savvy enough to reinvent themselves, from a marketing perspective, and to figure out how to connect emotionally to the changing consumer base that gets all its information through electronic media. The French châteaus have basically relied upon the same sales methods that were established during Napoleonic times, and communicating directly to the consumer has never before been a part of the equation—but now it has to be.

Once my new clients are ready to make the actual step of investing, I usually recommend they initially put down $25,000. This is basically the price of an economy car. If you wreck an economy car and it's a devastating blow to you financially, wine isn't the right investment for you. Look for a more traditional place to invest your money.

Instead, wine investing is for people who, if they happen to crash their car, can say, "Oh, well—I enjoyed driving it," and move on. Because worst-case scenario—from a financial standpoint—you might decide to drink all the wine from your initial investment, which will leave you happy but with nothing in your bank account to show for it. This has to be okay for you to do.

Typically, you shouldn't buy more than five twelve-bottle cases of any wine from a particular vintage when you're investing, because if you need to liquidate, it's harder to find takers when you're selling a lot of the same thing. And usually when someone is willing to buy large quantities of one product, they expect a discount for it. Another downside to high-volume purchases is that you're affecting the market by flooding it with one product when you sell all at once, which automatically drives the price down. If you keep a wide variety of premium vintages, you're more likely to see success when selling large quantities of wine at one time.

As with most types of investing, you always must have a mechanism for unloading your assets if you hit financial straits. With wine, it's a broker. I'll help you liquidate quickly—and I'm an expert who knows the markets, can tap into private collections, and can find the right buyers. You can't take a wine back to a premium retailer to resell it. They're in the business of selling a bottle to you once, and they aren't usually interested in reversing roles.

Never forget that wine investing is a real business. If you treat it like a passing hobby, you won't succeed. A $25,000 buy-in gives you enough leeway to experiment and learn the ups and downs of investing, without bottoming out. Your money will go farther, as I've said, when you work with a licensed, reputable broker who has a physical location and references, and who provides sound advice and will be held accountable to you.

My customers buy from me because they like me and they trust me. Because my business is small, we're flexible on commissions and aren't obsessively trying to meet sales goals. Establishing a rapport with a customer takes a long time and requires a significant investment on our part. We probably complete one out of every three deals with a customer without my company seeing a profit. We follow this arrangement because it helps the client's bottom line, and it maintains our relationship. We treat our clients as partners. They're investing in wine, and we're investing in them.

Right now, Estate Wine Brokers has exclusive access to over $15 million in inventory among our clients. This is in addition to the connections we've built with industry insiders—among the producers, restaurants, auction houses, other brokers, sommeliers, négociants, distributors, and collectors. It's up to you, the prospective investor, to find a broker who will give you a fair deal on products and who will take care of you and pass along lucrative opportunities—and at the same time give you sound advice on when to sell profitably. From there, it's your prerogative on whether to act on the advice you're getting.

WINE STORAGE

You're ultimately responsible for storing your investment safely. Without proper cellaring, your wine can become worthless in short order. Storing rare wine requires long-term thinking that takes into account all worst-case scenarios. For starters, your storage facility should have a backup power supply if the electricity ever gets knocked out. And you need to ensure proper security.

If you have a wine cellar at home, it should have climate controls. It should also be somewhere windowless, where the temperature remains constant throughout the day, between 55 and 60 degrees, regardless of the season. Wine refrigerators aren't acceptable, because they vibrate. Wineries around the world use subterranean wine caves, which naturally maintain the correct temperature and humidity, but they're prohibitively expensive for most collectors.

If you live in a hurricane-prone location, consider keeping the bulk of your collection in an off-site facility that's less vulnerable to extreme weather events. For instance, people who live in coastal areas along the Gulf of Mexico and the Eastern Seaboard should probably look far inland. In these locations, even facilities with backup generators can be taken off-line when a massive storm hits, due to physical damage or extended outages.

When considering off-site storage facilities, stick to ones that are dedicated specifically to wine; don't choose places that simply have a wine-storing section in them. Dedicated facilities are better equipped with climate-monitoring systems and multiple redundancies to maintain power. The people who run these facilities usually collect wine themselves, understand the ins and outs of proper storage, and aren't trying to cut corners. You'll get a sense of security knowing that your important investments are in their hands and are properly insured. Among the best dedicated facilities are the Manhattan Wine Company in New York and Imperial Wine Storage in West Palm Beach, Florida, to name two.

UNICORN WINES

There's a relatively new term in the industry: "unicorn wines." You'll see this hashtag on Twitter and references to it in wine publications. As its name implies, a unicorn wine is an extremely rare, highly sought-after bottle that you'll be lucky to see—and taste—once in your lifetime. It doesn't have to be pricey, necessarily, although it usually is.

There are no set criteria for what a unicorn wine is, though some people say that it has to have a production of less than four thousand cases, and that it can only be found through brokers and collectors and not listed online on Wine Searcher. They're basically cult wines that are in high demand—they're unique, and they have an intriguing story behind them. Oftentimes, you can find yourself wondering why, exactly, a unicorn is so popular.

Château Lafite Rothschild is the most obvious unicorn, becoming one when it reached a fever pitch in popularity in Asia in the early 2000s. The price of the wine rose from $150 on release to $1,500 within a couple of years because of the demand, but values quickly corrected when the market changed in the following years. Even if you sold Lafite today that you purchased ten to fifteen years ago, you'd still do well, just not as well as you could have done if you sold the wine between 2008 to 2013 when Lafite was on its upward tear.

Closer to home, the winery Sine Qua Non from California's Central Coast regularly produces what millennials call unicorn wines. The owner and winemaker is Manfred Krankl, a motorcycle-riding former sommelier and restaurant owner from Los Angeles. *Forbes* once called Sine Qua Non's products "the most coveted California wine you've never heard of." There's a six-year waiting list just to get onto their mailing list. Sine Qua Non makes a variety of potently high-in-alcohol craft wines, and they give each vintage a new name and label design. In 2014, a bottle of their 1995 rosé, called the Queen of Hearts, sold for $37,200 at auction.

What's head-scratching about the high prices Sine Qua Non's bottles can fetch is that the winery's products aren't long-term cellar wines. They basically make nonvarietals, which usually only cellar well for a decade, at most. Rosé, like that 1995 that sold for the equivalent of seven months' wages for the average American worker, is supposed to be consumed within three years of release. But for some reason, the Queen of Hearts had so much hype around its name, packaging, design, and backstory that it became a highly sought-after commodity. Usually people wouldn't spend $30 on a rosé, let alone $300 or $30,000. I'm not going to advise people to invest in rosé, especially one that's well beyond its expiration date.

Another domestic unicorn maker is the tiny Screaming Eagle winery in Napa. They're probably the first cult winery to emerge in California. They don't have the fabled history like nearby Ridge Monte Bello or Heitz Martha's Vineyard, but they do make great wine.

Created by a former real estate agent in 1986, Screaming Eagle sits on less than sixty acres and produces only four hundred to five hundred cases a year. Its 1992 Cabernet Sauvignon was given 99 points by Robert Parker, which drove demand for it to the moon. They only sell directly to the consumer, and they limit sales to three bottles per person a year. The waiting list just to get on their mailing list is thousands of names long.

ONE BROKER'S ROAD TO WINE

Being a wine broker sometimes feels like being a treasure hunter. It certainly did when I found myself in a private cellar in Miami in 2013. I was there because someone had defaulted on the property's lease, and the landlord—who got my name from an auction house—asked me to take a look at what was inside. The landlord didn't know anything about wine or the wine business, and he was just hoping to recoup his losses on rent as quickly as possible. He regarded the inventory in the wine cellar as little more than salvaged value from a real-estate deal gone bad.

For every exceptional trove of rare wines I find, I track down scores of false leads, so I was initially dubious about what would be inside. To my surprise, there were some beautiful, very rare wines among the two hundred bottles in this collection, and—just as importantly—they were in fabulous condition. The best of the lot was a 1985 Domaine Jacques-Frederic Mugnier Musigny, which was produced from Pinot Noir grapes from a famous twenty-five-acre vineyard in the Burgundy region of France. Among the others were some bottles of 1989 Domaine Dujac Clos de la Roche and a 1999 Domaine Rene Engel Echezeaux. Jackpot!

The landlord didn't want to waste time at auction with the bottles and was eager to make a deal. Additionally, the auction house had no history on the wine, so they could not auction it. He basically named his price, and I accepted, buying the wine for twenty-five cents on the dollar of its value. I paid him in cash on the spot, and I immediately arranged for a refrigerated truck to pack up the bottles and ship everything to the buyer's home.

After I left the property, I began scrolling through contacts on my cell phone for prospective buyers. I knew that among my large client base there would be any number of people eager to purchase the cellar's entire contents. It didn't take long for me to find exactly the right man.

Before the truck even crossed the state border, I sold the entire collection to a hedge fund manager who had worked with me in the past. He paid $65,000, which was about a $35,000 savings off retail market pricing.

In the end, everyone in the deal won. The landlord quickly recouped a portion of his real-estate losses, without fuss or hassle. The hedge fund manager was drinking rare wine that cost him one-third below retail and was elated at the amazing price. Later, he sold about a quarter of the collection at full value and made himself a profit. Then there was me: I was able to once again successfully do a job I love, hunting for a rare and valuable commodity made from grapes, and make an honest, profitable deal.

My personal wine journey began in an unlikely place: North Africa. I was born in Dallas, but my father's work in the oil business took me and my family to England shortly afterward. Then, when I was four years old, we moved to Tunisia. My parents are habitual collectors by nature. In England, it was antiques. In Tunisia, it was ancient Roman artifacts.

My father is Egyptian-born, and he has a fascination for historical relics that runs deep in his family. His brother, for a while, was the Vice Minister of Antiquities in Egypt. During our time in Tunisia, my father helped fund the archaeological digs performed by a local university. The country has been a crossroads of culture for well over three thousand years. It was ruled at different times by the Phoenicians, Romans, Arabs, Ottomans, and French. The city of Carthage was once considered the heart of all commerce on the Mediterranean. As a result, there's an incredible amount of history and culture buried just below the ground's surface throughout the country—much of it still waiting to be discovered.

When I lived in Tunisia there wasn't really any TV. So there were no shows or cartoons for a kid like me to obsess over, or sports to watch. Instead I had to find other ways to entertain myself. One of my favorites was to tag along with my dad when he visited the dig sites or met with local archaeologists. I was amazed by the artifacts, these treasures from the ground, and I'd lose myself in imagining the lives of the people who owned and used them, hundreds and sometimes even thousands of years ago.

My dad would often explain to me the significance of objects at digs, and he'd explain their origins and histories. He would point out whether the original owner of a plate or piece of cookware was a slave or noble, based on the type of clay used and the style of its molding. He'd show me the stamps placed on the bottoms of clay vessels that revealed the name of the person who actually made them.

Walking alongside my dad on these adventures was like being next to a college professor. There was no other place I wanted to be. I didn't really have anything else better to do, anyway, besides walk to the beach with my buddies. Of all the items he and I examined together, wine jugs and drinking vessels were the most common.

Wine in Tunisia dates back to the Phoenicians, and some of the same farming and grape-growing techniques that were first mastered more than one thousand years ago are still practiced today. The region's warm, dry climate is ideal for winemaking, and Tunisia employs mostly the same grape varieties as those in southern France, including Grenache, Syrah, and Merlot, though modern production is relatively modest. What's mostly lacking there is expertise. These countries are not necessarily large consumers of alcohol due to the prohibitions of the Islamic faith.

My initial interest in wine stemmed from this fascination with archaeology, but it was also cultivated at home, through my mother, who bought cases of high-end wine that were shipped to us from France. In my family, everyone respected and appreciated wine. No one pointed a finger at me and said, "You can't drink until you're twenty-one!" Instead, I was told, "Hey, try this Bordeaux with your meal." Or, "Have a sip of this Pinot Noir so you can understand culturally what it is, and how it changes the taste of the food."

Wine was a ritual at my dinner table, and as I got older, it became more of a hobby of mine—as an object to collect more than a beverage to drink—enmeshed with my interest in artifacts and archaeology. I lost track of wine as a teenager when my family moved back to Texas. After high school, I enrolled at the University of Texas at Austin, where the only time I thought about alcohol was when I wanted to party with my friends. Cheap beer was my poison of choice.

One time when I was home on college break, I got really drunk on some garbage booze—and my dad, upon seeing me, got really disappointed. He was disappointed over my condition but was more upset that I'd been drinking cheap liquor. He told me, "I have this wine cellar with all this amazing wine in it, some of finest alcohol made in the world. If you ask me, I'll pour some for you and let you try it. But instead you're going out and drinking garbage. It's like you have no class."

The words stung, and stayed with me, even though I didn't really change my habits. At least not until my junior year, when I went dove hunting in the Texas Hill Country with a fraternity brother and stopped at a local winery on the way back. We tasted a surprisingly amazing red blend, and memories from my days in Tunisia flooded back to me. I thought about all of those evening meals at the family dinner table. This was another "aha!" moment for me.

From that point forward, I stopped drinking beer and became one of those wine-drinking guys in college. None of my buddies or fraternity brothers gave me a hard time about it, and I'd say my dating life actually improved, since drinking wine made me seem more mature and sophisticated.

During my senior year, I was bitten by the entrepreneurial bug—which I would later combine with my affinity for wine to form the two businesses I own today. My merchandise at that time was Cuban cigars, which I started selling to make extra cash. Cigars were in fashion then, and people like Madonna and David Letterman were gracing the cover of *Cigar Aficionado*.

It was really easy for me to buy the cigars from credible sources that brought them back from Cuba. In turn, I'd sell them to stockbrokers, lawyers, and doctors—not to mention fellow students. I'd do something like start a poker game, pull out the cigars, and immediately build up a client list. I never considered the business a long-term venture, but it gave me a little money.

As a senior in college in 1999, I got an internship at a stock brokerage and began working behind the cage. This was during the dot-com boom, and I was fortunate to make a good bit of money in just a few short years. I didn't love the work, though, so I was always trying to think up new potential business ideas—often bouncing them off my buddies for their insight and advice—as an alternative route for my career that could potentially put me more in control of my own destiny.

During one of these mini-brainstorming sessions with friends, my roommate Aaron Bulkley (and co-founder of Personal Wine) suggested we start a personalized wine company. His idea was that we could take premium wine produced in the Texas Hill Country, bottle it, and produce custom wine labels for businesses to use as gifts for employees and customers. My reaction was, "Yeah, man, that sounds like fun."

We researched the concept on the Internet and discovered that no one was providing a similar service at that time. Bonus! So in 2000, we launched Personal Wine. During the first month of operations, we sold more than $15,000 worth of wine, mostly to stockbrokers I knew personally. Operations grew quickly from there. I became more invested in it—financially, time-wise, and emotionally—and we started developing a market that no one even knew existed to that point.

When I use the term "personalized" with respect to wine, most people think we're producing wine on demand or blending it to people's tastes. That's a misconception. The only thing we personalize is the packaging. At Personal Wine (www.personalwine.com), we let the winemakers do their thing, and we just make the bottles more attractive. All we do is add custom labels and engrave wine bottles with personalized messages. Personal Wine has grown into the number-one wine-gifting company in the country.

Even though I was confident that the company would be a success long-term, there were definitely doubters, even among my friends and family. One of my college fraternity brothers who was studying for his MBA called me shortly after I was getting Personal Wine off the ground. He asked if he and some fellow classmates could study my company as a class project and prepare an analysis of its future potential. I agreed.

Over the course of the next several months, they created a parallel hypothetical company to mine, using my basic business plan, while I was getting things off the ground. They developed financials, performed a SWOT (strengths, weaknesses, opportunities, and threats) analysis, created a financial plan, and extrapolated what the results would be. At the end of the semester, they showed me their final fifty-page document. Their conclusion: I had an 88 percent chance of failure. I was a little angry about the report, but I didn't dwell on it because I was too busy trying to run Personal Wine in the real world. In my mind, an 88 percent chance of failure meant there was, in fact, a 12 percent chance of success, and that was enough motivation for me.

The biggest hurdle for the company at that time was the ambiguity in laws surrounding the personalization of wine labels and bottles in Texas. We quickly discovered that we needed to find a lobbyist to help create a common-sense legal framework that could be proposed to the legislature and heads of the alcohol regulatory agency. Otherwise, we wouldn't know what laws to follow, and the state wouldn't know what to enforce. In other words, risk would remain high.

I was referred to Charles Bailey, a former special assistant criminal district attorney and chief of staff of Lieutenant Governor Bob Bullock, who was a fixture in the Texas legislative community. Chuck, as I call him, told me he was willing to help. He had always wanted to start his own entrepreneurial venture, and Personal Wine kind of gave him a way to experience it vicariously.

Chuck was an invaluable resource in locating a clear path through the political and legal maze surrounding selling personalized wine—and in creating a business structure that would work with the regulators. In the process, he became a close personal friend. Chuck Bailey is also an accomplished author on subjects surrounding political memorabilia.

When we launched Personal Wine, I wanted to be a local hero of sorts by finding a new market across the country for Texas wines. At that time, people didn't think of vintages from the Lone Star State as being anything special. It was more of a novelty. But the wine industry was for real in Texas then, and it is even stronger now. Wineries in Texas have stepped up their game, attracting world-class winemakers who are producing some amazing wines. I wanted the rest of the country to know about it.

Despite my ambitions, the idea of exclusively offering Texas wines at Personal Wine turned out to be a mistake. No one outside of Texas at that time wanted wine made in Texas, even if it was personalized. In some ways, it reinforced what my buddy's business school class had told me in their report. Their "88 percent chance of failure" notion was largely based on the fact that I'd be trying to peddle Texas wine. So I pivoted, and Personal Wine began using products from California and France. And with that development, the company began to achieve rapid growth that continues today.

The next obstacle was the difficulty of convincing recognizable wineries to sell their wine through the still-unknown personalized market, comingling their branded labels with personalized designs. They saw no incentive or upside, because business was so strong for their premium wines using their own branding. The only success we found came from wineries that were unable to sell their wines through traditional channels and were sitting on massive overstocks. It was like a scavenger hunt, and it wasn't an easy task.

To compound the situation, due to the way the wine business is structured, we were forced to work mostly through traditional wholesale distributors, not the wineries themselves. Based on the rules stipulated by the Texas Alcoholic Beverage Commission, retailers are forbidden from purchasing wine directly from producers and must instead acquire product through wholesale distributors. For their part, local distributors didn't particularly like my personalized wine business because it was outside of their normal business model. In short, it was too much of a hassle for them.

Distributors also saw us as a risk. They worried that if they arranged to buy large quantities of wine for my company, and then we went out of business, they'd be on the hook for wine they couldn't sell to anyone else. So they required us to buy the wine up front, before we even had the customer orders lined up. We were placed in a near-impossible position. Wine, as you can imagine, is difficult to store. If we didn't correctly anticipate the tastes of our prospective customers, and how much they'd be willing to order, then we would have gone out of business.

Still, this tenuous system with distributors worked, and we started to make a profit and built up a solid client base—especially with big corporations that had large marketing budgets and liked our concept and product. Our relationship with distributors improved as we added a bottle-engraving service to our list of offerings. This allowed us to take a bottle of, say, Silver Oak Cabernet Sauvignon and engrave a custom logo on the glass portion of the bottle without having to alter the branded label.

Custom-engraved Silver Oak Cabernet Sauvignon became such a hit that the winery called us to inquire how we were able to operate so well, which turned into a relationship to help them with orders they could not fulfill themselves. One year we managed to get six hundred bottles of Silver Oak Alexander Valley Cabernet Sauvignon etched, shipped, and delivered for a party celebrating the one hundredth anniversary of Wrigley Field. This order was placed on December 5th and delivered by the 9th, during our most intense production season.

Despite these developments in our company, the financial crisis of 2008 radically transformed the way we did business. We enjoyed an amazing first half to that year, achieving 28 percent growth, and forecasted an additional 32 percent growth in the following six months. In the late summer, we took some huge holiday preorders and began buying the wine to meet the upcoming demand. When the stock market tanked in October 2008, a lot of our clients suddenly canceled their orders. Yet we still had to live up to our commitments with the wineries to buy the wine—because when you make a commitment in the wine business, you live up to it or your reputation is forever ruined.

We spoke to our customers who had canceled their orders and basically said, "Don't worry about it. We'll figure out what to do on our side." We really focused on retaining those clients, so that we could work with them again when the economy eventually returned to normal. To make matters worse at that time, the distributors had basically stopped providing us with wine that we could use to add custom labels. They thought the economic crisis would bring about the end of our business model, so they had to reduce their risk and focus on their normal market.

We had no choice but to start speaking directly to the wineries where we had placed our orders. We said, "Look, we're going to honor our commitment, but it may take us a little longer. What can you do to work with us?"

Some said, "No, you have to pay us right away." So we did. Others said, "We'll hold the product a little longer than we anticipated then; that's fine." And we came to arrangements with them.

The market circumstances forced us to make another important decision: we turned Personal Wine into an official, legal winery. Under Texas state law, we could classify the business in this way if we bottled a certain amount of wine ourselves. By "bottled," I mean we would buy the wine finished in bulk quantities and put it in bottles ourselves, instead of having the wineries do it. Under this arrangement, we could more freely connect with the wineries, without having to go through distributors. It immediately reduced our overhead and eased our difficulties with distributors. From that point on, our relationship with distributors transferred from buying personalized wine to buying fine and rare wines for Estate Wine Brokers.

We also shifted our customer focus to adapt to the economic situation. Previously, we relied heavily on bigger, publicly held companies. But they no longer had marketing dollars to spend on personalized wine. A surprising number of small and midsized companies did, though.

Even with the financial crisis, private equity companies from Wall Street were still investing in them, and marketing dollars were still being spent among them. We began researching potential clients who had just raised a lot of private equity cash, and we aimed our sales efforts at them.

Yet another opportunity arose through the wineries themselves. They were sitting on a glut of product. Some tried the "flash sale" route, which involved selling off stocks directly through Groupon, Wines 'Til Sold Out, and other online outlets. But this setup created a problem, because it lowered the perceived value of the wine being sold, which estates didn't want to do. My company offered a different approach. We said, "We'll help you sell off your wine, and we can help you maintain your brand's value at the same time." We proposed to buy their excess premium wines and sell them through our personalized channels.

Through this arrangement, we could carve out a niche with clients by offering higher-quality wines, and bail out struggling wineries at the same time. In this sense, we became heroes of the industry, and our efforts allowed us to create enduring relationships with winemakers, distributors, and customers alike.

This enormous transformation to our business model took a couple of years, and from 2008 until 2010, I wasn't taking a paycheck from the company. To generate an income for myself on the side, I started to buy and sell rare wine. I was finding that the financial crisis was forcing people to sell off large portions of their cellars and that there weren't many buyers. I was already an avid rare wine collector, so this type of investment seemed like a natural fit for me. Plus, I already had some experience in the field.

When I started Personal Wine in 2000, I noticed that often the big wine distributors weren't very organized with maintaining and correctly inventorying their port-folios. Bottles would often sit on the shelves in storage, and in the eyes of distributors, the longer a wine stays in inventory without being ordered by a retailer, the less value it has (regardless of how valuable the bottle actually is).

Occasionally, I'd find rare wines that were misspelled or misnamed on product lists, so other retailers didn't know they were available among a distributor's inventory. I'd spot them, wait until they hit the list of closeout specials, and then buy everything on the list. All of it. By investing a couple of thousand dollars, I would acquire wines worth $100 or $200 per bottle for as little $10 or $20 per bottle. Some I'd save, some I'd drink, and others I'd sell for profit at auctions or to friends or acquaintances.

The money I made often went back into the business expenses for Personal Wine. I'd think to myself, *This will buy me equipment for the office*. But my buying and selling was more of a hobby, a small side venture.

I didn't fully enter into the wine brokerage business until 2010, and it happened partly by accident. My first sale was a 1945 Château Mouton Rothschild. I bought it from a billionaire wine collector for $7,500. It's one of those once-in-a-lifetime bottles, rated 100 points by Robert Parker. It was made in the winery's return to production after the Allied victory in Europe. The label reads "Year of Victory" in French, and many would argue that this was perhaps the greatest wine in all of the twentieth century.

Ironically, I wasn't even planning on selling the bottle. For just about my entire life to this point, I had dreamed of collecting that one bottle, the pinnacle of all wines, and this was it. My intent was to save it for some big milestone—some important accomplishment or moment when I could open it to celebrate with a few close friends and savor it.

Shortly afterward, however—before I even came into possession of the bottle, which was being cellared in New York—I was told that a certain movie star was interested in buying it from me, and price wasn't an issue. Through the star's representatives, we agreed on a price, which would make me a handsome profit. I agreed to the deal, despite how much I had dreamed of opening a bottle like this one, and said I would hand-deliver it, to ensure the integrity of the chain of custody.

Within days, I was in New York, a bottle of 1945 Château Mouton Rothschild in hand, packing it with extra padding in a Styrofoam box to protect it from harm in the luggage compartment of the airplane for my direct flight from New York to California. I took the bottle directly to the movie star's business manager, and we concluded the deal. The whole experience got me hooked on brokering wine. It was such an exciting and interesting slice to the industry. Every day would be different.

Being an entrepreneur, I've never been interested in owning a standard retail wine store. I don't like being locked down to the same physical location and doing the same thing every day. I don't like repetitive situations. And with a wine store, you have to be on location all the time to be profitable, schmoozing with customers, giving the business a unique personality and the customers a reason to walk in the door.

Being a wine broker gives me variety. The work is always interesting and different. Not that it always reaps rewards, especially for people like myself who insist on being thorough about every aspect of the deal. Shortly after the sale of that Château Mouton Rothschild, I experienced the downside of the business. It happened in Florida.

I went to Miami to inspect some wine that came from a distribution company that went out of business. The two partners who owned it had a falling-out, and one took half of the inventory and dropped it at the warehouse of an import-export company in Miami. I arrived at the building to find that it wasn't insulated, and the temperature inside was probably 80 degrees. The first case of wine in the inventory that caught my eye was a 2004 Le Pin from the village of Pomerol in Bordeaux. Widely recognized as one of the finest estates in Bordeaux, a single bottle of Le Pin can sell for thousands of dollars. But not these, which were slowly baking in the heat of a Florida warehouse.

I looked around at the rest of the wine and felt as if someone had hit me in the gut. There were some amazing Bordeaux in the collection, all in the original wood boxes. The owner of the import-export business held all the invoices from the original purchase order. But the goods were worthless.

"How long have you kept these boxes here?" I asked him. Eight months, he replied. I opened one of the Le Pin crates, and it looked like a murder had taken place inside the box. Wine had been seeping out of the bottles because of the pressure inside from the heat. It didn't help that this man had put a fan on top of these wood boxes, triggering vibration, which caused the seeping wine to spray all over the place.

The import-export owner said, "No problem, we'll just clean the bottles and they'll be fine."

My response was, "Well, that's not exactly how it works."

He said, "I know the wines are fine. Every once in a while, I'll pull one out and drink it and it tastes fine."

Oh, my lord.

I told him that regardless of how they tasted, I couldn't sell them as premium products. In fact, I didn't feel comfortable selling them at all—even "as is, buyer beware." My feeling was that no matter who bought them, they weren't going to be happy in the end, because chances were that a large percentage of the bottles were going to be maderized, a process whereby wine is heated to the point of oxidization. Not to mention the fact that the buyer would be forced to drink them all within the next six to twelve months, because any increase in temperature of a bottle can greatly accelerate the aging process of the wine contained within.

When I told the import-export owner all of this, he got really pissed off at me. He offered to sell the entire inventory for 50 percent off. I replied that I couldn't even offer ten cents to the dollar. I had to walk away from the situation, quickly.

My mission as a wine broker has been, and always will be, to provide an amazing, honest service. I do this by minimizing risk for all parties involved, by doing my homework and being meticulous in every detail. Integrity is essential in these transactions. I couldn't have stayed true to myself, my clients, or the fundamental philosophy behind my business if I had tried to sell those bottles.

I'm probably held to an even higher standard for transparency because the two businesses I own stretch me in different directions in the wine industry. For that reason, I essentially keep a firewall between them. I've been the victim of fraud—where someone has taken an inferior wine, placed it in a bottle, forged a label for it, and sold it for a high price as a rare wine—so the last thing I want is to be falsely accused of committing an act of this type myself.

At Personal Wine, we select wines from our partner wineries and personalize the labels that get affixed to the bottles.

We do this for special occasions for people, as well as for companies celebrating holidays or who want to give the wine away as client gifts. Our labels are printed digitally, not offset printed like the ones on rare wines, and they're produced on demand. We have records of every single transaction that we've had with every client. Our business is intentionally kept as open as possible so there are no misunderstandings or discrepancies.

With Estate Wine Brokers, it's my job to track down and verify the history and chain of custody—or provenance—of every bottle I help sell, and provide this information to the client. I follow the trail of ownership and transportation all the way back to the producer. This type of background check helps ensure the quality of the wine by uncovering not only where it has been stored since it was first sold, but how and under what climate conditions. We also offer insurance through Aon Insurance and a couple of other providers, which covers the transaction.

While no countermeasures are perfect when it comes to detecting fraud, if any potential red flags do arise when I'm investigating a bottle, I'll err on the side of caution and walk away from the deal. Risks aren't worth taking in the rare wine business. I remember one time when I looked at a parcel of magnums of 1985 Henri Jayer Echezeaux Grand Cru. Made in Burgundy, this vintage generally sells for more than $5,000 a bottle. These bottles are difficult to find and incredibly desirable. I made a couple of phone calls and found that the original owners were people who had once shared connections with a convicted wine counterfeiter. Even though the provenance wasn't in question, I thought the dots connected a little too closely together and didn't want to take any chances.

Another time, I went to inspect the wine collection of a wealthy, prominent person before he had it checked by an authenticator. He wanted to convert some of his bottles into quick cash. I examined a handful of them and knew that it was impossible for those wines to be together in the same place at the same time. It was a dream team of the most well-known and hardest-to-get vintages in the world. In other words, the contents of his cellar were just too good to be true—like a random mansion having a Picasso, Monet, Warhol, and Jackson Pollock together hanging on the walls. So I steered myself clear of the inventory.

In addition to being thorough in my transactions as a wine broker, I'm also incredibly candid. Nobody wants or appreciates surprises in this business, and that means that I have to provide realistic expectations. When our clients at Estate Wine Brokers are selling a bottle, we don't give broad ranges of potential prices. Instead, we give them one or two—maybe sometimes three—options, and then try to find a price they select. Either we perform or we don't, and that bottle won't leave their possession unless we perform. Clients appreciate this kind of straightforward approach.

When purchasing wine for our customers, we always want them to get the maximum value—not only through the price of the bottle, but also through the services we provide. This includes the disclosures about the provenance of the wine, and the warranty, and the fact that we've got a track record of success and reliability.

People know that we're in business for the long haul, not the quick score, and that we'll sacrifice short-term gains in order to protect the reputation of integrity and trustworthiness that we've spent more than a decade cultivating. Estate Wine Brokers receives more than 95 percent of its new business through referrals, and I'm determined to make sure its good name is never compromised.

Before there was Robert Parker, there was Denman Moody, a former banker and financial consultant from Houston, Texas, who began writing about wine in the early 1970s. There's no one more famous or knowledgeable in the Houston, Texas, wine-collecting circles than him. During his lifetime, he has rubbed elbows with the who's who of most powerful Texans.

One day a few years back, he called me and told me of a real-estate developer friend who had passed away. The man had once owned a large wine collection, but he sold all of it at auction before he died, except for twelve bottles that were still being kept by his widow. Moody wanted me to take a look at them. He said the wines had impeccable provenance and that he'd vouch for them. He has never been one who has wanted—or needed—to make a quick buck, and I hold him in high regard, so I agreed.

Moody told me to meet him at a house in the Memorial neighborhood in Houston. When I arrived, he showed me the collection, and I was instantly blown away. If you could make a list of "Top Ten Wines to Taste before You Die," most of the wines in front of me would be on it. And they were in impeccable condition. The first to catch my eye was a 1961 Château Latour Bordeaux, which Robert Parker gave a 100 score. I also saw a couple of 1945 Latours; a 1964 Petrus Pomerol, which earned a 99 Robert Parker score; and a 1961 Château Lafite Rothschild.

I've seen suspect bottles before and generally know what to look for. I know which vintages started selling when, and what the capsules of bottles look like. These looked completely authentic. Moody said, "I've known the owners for more than thirty years and have witnessed these bottles in their collection the whole time."

Regardless, I inspected them as thoroughly as possible, and I photographed them for reference.

Moody told me that the widow wanted to sell them, quietly and without fuss, and without any desire to ever meet the buyer. He said she doesn't drink anymore and is never in the country. Then he asked me if I wanted to buy them. My response: "Of course." We negotiated a price right there, then drove to the bank, and I gave him the money. Later that day I took the wine back to Austin with me, and within twenty-four hours I had found a buyer.

I actually drank one of the 1945 Latours with the client who bought it. Just popping the cork and smelling the wine in the guy's closed wine cellar was amazing. I thought about how, just after World War II was ending, and humanity was emerging from one of the darkest eras in its history, the Bordelaise so quickly produced such remarkable wine.

Frankly, I was surprised that the Latour had also kept so amazingly well. The flavor was very youthful, the tannins were finessed, and the acidity and fruit were still there. It had intensity and body, like Audrey Hepburn in a bottle. This was definitely one of my top five moments as a wine broker. It encapsulated why I'm in the business.

I truly consider myself a treasure hunter. However, instead of having of a setup like American Pawn, where I sit behind a counter and people bring me all kinds of amazing stuff to see, I'm actually on the road, going to places, seeking out rare finds. On a Monday I may be sorting through a cellar in Washington, DC, and the next day I'm in Chicago, and the day after that in Los Angeles before returning home for breakfast by Thursday morning. Hunting for treasures means sometimes hitting the big cache and sometimes striking out. Regardless, the experiences are never dull.

The greatest lesson this business has taught me is to be patient and disciplined. I play the long game, knowing that down the road the rewards will be greater, both financially and personally. The industry is small, chatter among insiders spreads fast, and trust has to be earned. My reputation is my most valuable, and delicate, asset and something that I can't compromise under any circumstance.

Collecting rare wine isn't really a quick-fix, day-trading type of pursuit, anyway. It's built more on predicting long-term trends through knowledge, business sense, research, and vision. It also requires passion. You have to love wine, for its historic and cultural value, and its artistic qualities. There's no better feeling than putting a rare bottle of wine in the hands of someone who will appreciate it as much as I do.

CONCLUSION

———

Wine is different from so many other investable assets because it's more like a work of art than a commodity. Serge Hochar, a legendary winemaker who tragically passed away in 2015, pointed this fact out to me. His family's winery, Château Musar, produces some of the greatest wines in the world, from the unlikely location of the Bekaa Valley in Lebanon, near the Syrian border. His father studied grape growing and winemaking in Bordeaux in the 1930s, and he sold his first vintages to the French military officers and diplomats stationed in Beirut prior to World War II, when Lebanon was still under French control.

Serge took over the winery in the late 1950s, and then, when the civil war broke out in the 1970s and 1980s, he kept producing, even with artillery bombarding the vineyards and the roads often barricaded. The opposing sides of the fighting would stop bombing to allow him to tend to his vineyards, and his people clothed themselves in flak jackets during harvest.

I saw Serge at a wine event a few years back, when he made this allusion to me about wine and art: "With wine, you have the land, you have the climate. God gives you these pieces, and then you need to assemble them into this perfect singular event of something that you pour into a glass. Wine is art." This profound quote really sticks with me, even today. That's what he taught me.

The more I thought about it, the more I agreed with what he said. With a painting, you have a canvas and paint, but the artist has to take those two pieces and put them together and create an expression that the world has never seen before and will appreciate. Making wine requires that same painstaking process, involving immense skill, practice, patience, creativity, talent, ingredients, and finally, a ton of chemistry. The only difference with wine is that the end product is more fleeting, since it's consumable.

I realized after listening to Serge that people invest in wine for the same reason they would invest in an expensive painting, or spend $500 to $1,000 to eat at a world-class restaurant where there's a waiting list that's two years long.

They'll do it for the unique experience that's as much emotional as it is a financial transaction. People who drink and love wine can easily transition that passion into the wine business. If they're a professional—a Wall Street trader, a doctor, or a lawyer, for instance—and they're earning over $75,000 per annum, investing in wine enables them to be knowledgeable about a part of their assets, even if it's only a small amount. They can feel more in control.

Investing in Wall Street sits on the opposite end of the spectrum from investing in wine. In this case you're basically giving someone money and saying, "Go make me more money." If you invest in or collect wine, however, whether it's in a cellar or storage facility, your job is to store it and maintain its value (unless, of course, you have your broker do this). The wine is your baby. You'll be the one making sure the temperature is controlled at a steady 55 to 62 degrees Fahrenheit. You'll make sure that the humidity is 55 to 65 percent, and that there's no mold infestation in your house. You'll also be looking to store the wine away from direct sunlight. You'll be the one ultimately gauging the value of your wine and deciding when or if you want to sell it.

This is how I approach investing in wine, and I hope this book has helped you understand if you should do it, and then how to do it if you choose to.

I live and work in Austin, Texas, but I travel extensively and always like to meet fellow wine lovers and investors. If you would like to meet up and possibly share a glass of wine, email me at alex@personalwine.com, and let's set it up.

ABOUT THE AUTHOR

ALEX ANDRAWES is the founder and executive chairman of Pervino Inc., a wine conglomerate based out of Austin, Texas, whose subsidiaries include Personal Wine, the #1 personalized wine shop in the USA, and Estate Wine Brokers, a brokerage firm specializing in rare, investment-grade wine sourced from privately owned cellars. Andrawes founded Personal Wine his senior year at the University of Texas at Austin and entered the brokerage business in 2010, when he scored a rare 1945 Chateau Mouton Rothschild. Since then, he has formed an international viticultural network, sourcing, trading, and sharing unbelievable vintages with wine aficionados across the globe.

Printed in Great Britain
by Amazon

People who work to improve their lives are always trying to change their thoughts. By doing this, it becomes easier for the mind to evolve and grow. It is through your emotional problems that one learns what can be done to get the problems one has managed. Cognitive psychology is a practice that helps people to understand how to thrive in life and make the work one puts in worthwhile. With CBT, a person will have more control over your thoughts. Because someone knows how to manage the positive ones and to keep the negative issues in your mind from being a dramatic threat, the thoughts will be easy to manage. The fears that one might experience can be alleviated through CBT. The practice allows anyone to think twice about the fears one has and how they can hinder your way of living a comfortable life. This includes an emphasis on knowing how fears are formed and how to gradually correct them before they can become a burden.

CBT also works to relieve anxiety and for a person to recognize how irrational some anxiety-related triggers are. Many fears are not as strong as one might think and the anxieties produced by them are not things to be concerned about. Some of the saddest feelings can be managed through CBT. When the right ideas for regulating the mind and your thoughts are introduced, depression does not have to be a burden. Grief can be kept in check by using some constructive points and smart ideas to move on with life and to keep grief from crippling your way of living.

People Talk About Your Need for a Psychiatrist

Even when someone tries to do things and change their thinking, they might still have many visible problems that others may notice. It is through your emotional problems that one learns what can be done to get the problems one has managed. The thoughts will be easy to manage because they know how to thinks positive ones and to keep the negative issues in your mind from being a dramatic threat. The practice allows anyone to think twice about the fears one has and how they can hinder your way of living a comfortable life. Every instance of how CBT may work varies by person, so knowing what to expect out of the process will be essential to your success in keeping your life in check.

Chapter 13 - Living a Healthy Lifestyle

Sleep

There are things you will do in your life outside the CBT methods that may greatly help your well-being and increase the effectiveness of any therapy you utilize. One vital factor is sleep. Having enough sleep is important for mood, energy levels, physical ˙health, and even the health of the brain. Things like anxiety will make it difficult to sleep, making a reinforcing cycle of stress and exhaustion. However, there are several straightforward changes you'll create to help yourself get a decent night's sleep, such as attempt to sleep and wake up at a similar time every day and to sleep after you feel tired. Don't oversleep to make up for lost sleep. Don't watch TV, use your phone, or dine in bed. Offer yourself thirty minutes to an hour before bed to relax. Get physical activity throughout the day, it could help you sleep better at night.

Healthy Eating

Many of us realize that a healthier diet contributes to a more robust sense of overall well-being. It can even contribute to weight loss and improvement of different health factors,

relieving anxiety within the method. If you're feeling that addressing your diet currently would result in a lot of anxiety, leave it for a later time. However, if you're feeling driven to enhance your diet, go for it. It may be the thing you need to feel healthier and less anxious or depressed. You should merely aim to eat a lot of fruit, vegetables, whole grains, fish, healthy fats like oil and avocado, nuts, and seeds, and less white meat, high-fat dairy farm, white flour and refined grains, sugars, change oils, and processed foods generally. If you love cooking, taking cooking lessons and creating healthier home-cooked meals may well be a good a part of your behavioral-activation strategy.

Physical Activity

Physical activity is the simplest way to enhance mood. Physical activity doesn't have to mean exercise. Many of us believe that they need to move to the gym and run on a treadmill or ride a stationary bike for it to count. This is mostly not true! There are several other ways to be active that doesn't involve going to the gym. Walking, biking, and hiking outside is fun and restful, and many believe that walking and standing more can help you live a longer life.

Low-intensity activities like gardening, playing catch together with your kid, doing yard work, or actively cleaning the house up are great options.

Meditation

Meditation could be a good way to alleviate stress and cultivate attentiveness. There are several approaches that can be used. One simple option is to begin a mantra meditation. It's a type of meditation during which one chooses a sound or phrase and repeats it for a number of times. It is as straightforward as a soothing sound, like "om" or "ahh," or it is a phrase in any language expressing sentiments of compassion, kindness, or peace. You'll need to make one up yourself or use a conventional ancient mantra that has been murmured for hundreds of years. There's extremely nice flexibility in mantra meditation. Make sure to choose a mantra that is soothing and can assist you in clearing your mind throughout meditation. If you are interested in mantras and meditation, there are several videos online that may assist you in providing you with the proper methods and meditation examples.

If you want, you could shift to silent meditation. For those that follow a religion, repetitive contemplation of any prayer or passage from scripture is very effective. Select any passage from your holy book. You can read or chant it repeatedly. While you do that, make sure to relish every word and each phrase. Take the time to hear yourself as you recite the passage. What insights and reflections will it awaken in you? Watch your response to your prayer, and after you are done, pay attention to yourself in complete silence. To get the most out of your

mediation, try to it on a daily basis. Attempt to put aside ten to fifteen minutes every day to try other kinds of mantra meditation. If you can't, that's okay. Just do the best that you can.

Nature Therapy

Recent studies have found that interacting with nature on a daily basis has a tremendous impact on our sense of health, happiness, and well-being. You don't have to do any intense running or hiking, you could just sit in a pretty clearing, or sketching a beautiful scene in the nature around you. Getting sun and fresh air has a major effect on stress levels. If you reside close to a forest, like a state park, put aside an hour or so for a visit. If not, you'll get similar benefits from a town park with trees and a green grass. It doesn't specifically have to be a forest either. A meadow, a big backyard, a river, or any outside space you discover stunning and soothing can do. Create a way to immerse yourself within the outdoor space. Close up your phone or leave it in your car. Interact all of your senses within the experience. Take notice of the smell of the soil, the air, and plants, the sounds of wind, water, and animals, the feel of leaves and bark, and also the feel of the earth below your feet. Relish the brilliant colors and look at all the flowers, maybe even jots down the color and look of any you find particularly beautiful.

Bird-Watching

Bird-watching could be a tremendous way to get away. You can feel completely immersed within the experience of being outside since you're going to be really focused on every flash of color and each rustle or sound. It's precisely this type of complete interaction with nature that helps relieve stress and boost your everyday mood. It additionally helps you to marvel at nature, as you develop an appreciation for the various kinds of birds and their distinctive habits. If you're already a bird watcher, create a degree to travel out a least a number of times per month. Visit new locations, and listen to seasonal migrations that will offer you an opportunity to examine new birds. Bird watching is additionally a good activity to do on vacations since several stunning natural areas around the world boast numerous bird and wildlife as well as cater to bird watchers. Even if you haven't ever gone bird watching before, it's a straightforward hobby that is easy to get started with. All you'll have to need is some binoculars and either your phone or a book to help you identify the birds you see. Then head to a park, or maybe an oversized yard, and see what kinds of birds you'll see. Wherever you reside, you could possibly attract several kinds of birds with feeders you can hang near your home.

Disorders like anxiety and depression tend to be rampant in America. As people, we tend to become excessively focus on ourselves. This typically comes from being overwhelmed—the emotions that we tend to feel are unable to

influence our current reality. This could lead to emotional dysfunction within the face of things that aren't really threatening. Our individual worlds become nerve-racking and demand a lot of our attention. However, it doesn't mean that we are not generous or we tend to not care about other people. You are by no means a "bad person" for feeling like this! Being overwhelmed could be a common symptom of the many mental diseases and disorders. This intense self-focus could be a type of suffering caused by anxiety or depression and not merely an indication of selfishness. In fact, we tend to typically care deeply for the people we love and feel badly that we tend to not be as responsive or caring as we might wish to be. It becomes analytic, and isolation is excruciating for humans. Humans are naturally social creatures. We tend to relish the sense of happiness. We tend to be the most satisfied and we care deeply about the connections with others and their well-being.

Gaining perspective

There are great ways to gain perspective and feel better that complement CBT. Let's look at some examples of things that you can incorporate in your daily life to keep a positive perspective.

Nature

We've already talked regarding a number of the advantages of being in nature for stress reduction. Experiencing stunning sunsets, mountains, waterfalls, rolling waves, beautiful coastlines, big

trees, and wondrous animal life will cause you to feel connected to the rest of the living world. Think about the fact that the mountains you're standing on are there for thousands of years, that the tree lofty higher than you is formed from small cells distantly involving your own, or that the birds stopping to rest in your yard migrate thousands of miles will offer perspective and shift your focus from aspects of your life that you simply understand as negative. If you've got vacation time, create a plan to travel somewhere with natural beauty, whether or not it's on the opposite side of the globe or simply an hour away at a nature reserve. If you prefer exciting activities, do something exhilarating during a trip like mountain biking, paragliding, or windsurfing. Walking, hiking, cycling, horseback riding, or just resting within the presence of beautiful natural options will fill you with a sense of awe and place things in perspective. Looking at a visually beautiful documentary can even inspire a way of awe regarding nature.

Art and Music

The sweetness and depth of human expression through art and music is moving and awe-inspiring. Listen to singers whose voices you discover really distinctive and exquisite. Go to an opera or a symphony with an awesome, sweeping finale. Explore paintings and sculptures that are beautiful in their ability to capture feelings. Read poetry that touches you with its sincerity and creativeness. If no artists or artworks come to mind immediately, that's okay. Consider art and

music as a therapeutic path to explore, with the goal of discovering a number of creations that inspire you.

Chapter 14 - Problem Solving

Problem-solving is great when a circumstance can be changed, but that change might be laden with tension. Problems may likewise be associated with sadness, medical issues, drug and alcohol dependence, or family issues. Some sorts of problems that could be having no proper communication your life partner, paying off your bills, starting a new diet, or striving to stop smoking.

This methodology isn't proper for all problems. In the event that you are experiencing extreme sadness or genuine psychological instability, this methodology won't be sufficient for these issues. Now and again, there isn't an answer to every problem. Problem-solving will sometimes just give you ways of dealing with stress so that you will be able to live with it. This is called emotion-focused coping and it can help give you a more solid feeling of control and confidence. There are is a plan within CBT to help you with problem-solving. Let's look at CBT's approach.

The problem-solving approach educated with CBT has seven steps:

Step 1: Identify the Problem

The first step is to understand the problem in detail. Write down your problem and how you think your plan will fix that problem. Stick to the facts of the problem, so that your plan can be both actionable and reasonable.

Step 2: Identify Reasonable Plans

Think about your goals. Try not to worry about them being perfect. Just stay reasonable in your plans. If you do make some plans that later doesn't seem feasible, you can always change them down the road.

Step 3: Evaluate Your Plans

When you have a couple of realistic plans, record the advantages and disadvantages of each one. You can reach out to friends and family for help and feedback.

Step 4: Decide on Ideal and Backup Plans

In view of the advantages and disadvantages of the conceivable plans, settle on the best plan and a couple of backup plans.

Step 5: Plan What You Have to Do

Plan out the small steps involved in your plan. Separating it into little steps can make it more manageable.

Step 6: Carry Out Your Plan

Do the steps you recorded in Step 5. If necessary, move to one of your backup plans.

Step 7: Review and Change Plan as Required

How could it go? Is the problem solved decreased to a more reasonable level? If the problem isn't solved or if another problem has emerged, you can come back to Step 1 and figure another plan. You can do this as often as you need to.

The many things that have been covered in this guide deserve to be noticed. There are a few final tips that need to be discussed when aiming to get the most out of the cognitive behavioral therapy process.

Always Have a Goal

A clear-cut goal will include a clear objective. The goal can be anything that someone one wants to do so long as it is positive and reasonable. The goal can be a long-term or short one. The goal

must be clearly defined and realistic regardless of the type of situation that one encounters.

Every Situation Is Unique

Overgeneralization and other distortions are often things that people will encounter. These problems often make it harder for people to plan smart ideas or thoughts. People need to recognize that the situations are always different. People might look at the circumstances including a review of each situation based on the setting, the people who are involved, and any other things that might trigger changes. People should avoid personalizing the situations. Personalizing can disrupt your train of thought. Don't assume everything is about oneself.

Determine the Proper Definitions

Every attitude or emotion that one has will come with a distinct definition. When figuring out how well CBT can work, it is up to a person to recognize the certain definitions that one wishes to follow. A person might have your own idea for what disappointment is like. There could be a difference between the objectives that one has and the expectations involved. Understanding what disappointment is really like in your mind can be essential for handling your values and ideas. When resolving emotional problems, there is a need to think carefully about the definitions that will be used to ensure there are no problems with what one will be doing.

Never Blame Others

The goal of cognitive psychology is to help people recognize what they are doing for themselves and how they can be better people without being hard on others. Much of this involves ensuring that other people are not blamed for the things that one might do or say. It is very easy to pass off the responsibility of a situation to someone else. Blaming is a frequent practice that is easy to do, but it only shows a lack of responsibility. It suggests that instead of being willing to accept a situation for what it is, someone will instead think more about the problems that have developed. The best thing to do in this situation is to be accepting of whatever has come your way. It is not productive to blame others for everything that happens.

Never Be Overly Judgmental

It is understandable why people might be hard on themselves. They have their own worries or fears and they want to make what they are doing work well. The work that someone puts into CBT can only go so far as one wants it to go. Having a useful and smart plan on hand for therapy can make a real change in your life.

Conclusion

All of the points in this guide are suitable for many needs. They all require introspection and effort on a person's part to work. Those who are committed to the therapeutic process will find that it is not hard to get more out of the practice. Be aware of how much time and control it might take to resolve certain emotional issues. Look at the work being put into the process and see what can be done to manage life in a constructive fashion. Always be aware of the situation one enters into and how challenging the problem might be. Every instance of how CBT may work varies by person, so knowing what to expect out of the process will be essential to your success in keeping your life in check. Most importantly, be patient when using CBT. Every person responds to CBT uniquely. It might take weeks or even months to make cognitive progress. The effects of the process can last a lifetime and will allow a person to feel better about any situation one encounter. Good luck with using the points highlighted in this guide. When the best strategies and ideas for the concern are used, it is easy to keep fears, depression, and other negative aspects of your life from being overly influential.

Printed in Poland
by Amazon Fulfillment
Poland Sp. z o.o., Wrocław